Contents

Challenging Children to Chastity

— A Parental Guide —

by

H. Vernon Sattler, C.Ss.R.

Imprimi potest:	Edward J. Gilbert, C.Ss.R.
	Provincial Superior
	August 12, 1991

Nihil obstat: David A. Bohr, S.T.D.
Censor Librorum
August 14, 1991

Imprimatur: +James C. Timlin, D.D.
Bishop of Scranton, PA.
August 14, 1991

Scripture quotations are from the
New Revised Standard Version
Copyright 1989
Division of Christian Education
National Council of Churches of Christ in the USA.

Preface

Father H. Vernon Sattler, C.Ss.R. is a fine priest who has devoted most of his life to the task of being a theologian and educator. His contributions in the field of moral theology are diverse in subject matter, yet one in their adherence to the teaching of Jesus Christ. In the spirit of his patron, St. Alphonsus Ligouri, he has shown a passion for exploring and presenting the unity of doctrine and life.

It is no surprise, then, that he should make this contribution aimed at helping today's parents to covey the virtue of chastity to their children. What does come as a surprise, though, is that Fr. Sattler tells us to read this book and then forget about it. By design this is no ordinary "how to" manual. It is meant to be a source of leaven, a packet of yeast which is broken open and kneaded into the dough of daily living. The words of the book, the examples, the inferences are meant to remain obscure in themselves, but through their instrumentality the reader is to catch on to a new way of thinking about chastity education.

We live in an age when God's beautiful ennobling gift of human sexuality is so often trivialized and reduced to a mere primal drive for physical gratification having no inherent moral worth. In such an atmosphere, the breadth of what it means to truly love can be lost by a depersonalized or mechanically orientated approach to teaching our children about their role in the creative will of God. Fr. Sattler's rather unique method of unabashed and free flowing reflection and commentary is meant to challenge parents to go beyond the absorption of facts. He encourages them to embrace an entirely Catholic outlook in such a way that their children will "catch" it from them.

Our Holy Father has taught in the Apostolic Exhortation *Familiaris consortio* that parents are "called to offer their children a clear and delicate sex education" rooted in an "education to love as self-giving." [1] It is my sincere hope that many parents will draw upon this book as a resource to assist them in their lifelong task of self-giving love and that their children will come to know and do the truth in love.

John Cardinal O'Connor
Archbishop of New York

[1] *Familiaris consortio,* no. 37. Also cited in *Educational Guidance in Human Love* — Outlines for Sex Education, Sacred Congregation for Catholic Education, November 1, 1983.

Introduction

Please, do not read and study this book so as to pass a test. No examination can certify you as a good sex educator, or, better, an educator in chastity. There are no True-False answers, multiple choice tests, no grades. Education, speech fluency, literacy, inventiveness, have little to do with good sex or chastity education. True conjugal-parental love alone counts. Loving mistakes, fumbled and corrected, might be much more effective than technically perfect efforts. Professional teachers may have the degrees and class-room skills, but not necessarily the ability to instill virtue, or what Christian virtue presupposes, faith in Divine Revelation as certified in Christ through a teaching Church.

Do not, repeat, **do not**, memorize this material, utilize clever phrases, take notes from it, follow it as some sort of blueprint of good sex education. Please do not attempt to follow its logic, order or procedure. Above all, do not attempt to "repeat" even a single phrase for any one of your children. If you do you will sound phoney, like a puppet without a voice of its own, or a dull, mechanical, unconvincing recording. Only if you have made the thought and attitudes presented here your own with full personal conviction, should you try to repeat phrases.

Though there might be a correct way to impart Christian sex education, no one has ever done it correctly without mistakes! Parents confuse the issue. Children misunderstand. Sometimes it seems that they perversely and deliberately refuse to understand! Of course they do! With the awesome responsibility for sexual meaning, who wants to assume it too soon? Though you should try to avoid mistakes, often enough errors in positive or negative attitudes, whether in fact or truth, might be more important to the final result than doing it correctly in the first place, because once corrected, a error in belief or conviction might be all the more strongly compensated for. Often a broken bone is stronger because of the special healing demanded by the break. Yet, no one would deliberately break a bone to make it stronger!

Read this work. Start in the beginning, at the end, in the middle. Pick it up and read it where it falls open. Mull over what it says. Taste it. Roll it around on your tongue. Compare it with your general experiences. Add it to or subtract it from your living experiences and accumulated wisdom of success and failure.

Then forget it!

When your children ask questions, or show a need for information or formation you will not be able to recall the suggestions the book offers anyway. You will not be able to find the book to look them up, and if you can find it and do look up an answer, you will have lost the magic moment and the child or adolescent will have wandered off wondering why you made such a production of answering a simple question or puzzled attitude. Weren't you there when he was conceived? Born? When did you last research the answer to a question on safe driving, honesty, patriotism, loving your parents, helping the poor, respecting your clergyman, telling the truth, honestly filling out your income tax form, being loyal to your team or school or ethnic customs, obeying the traffic cop, brushing their teeth, table manners? This book is deliberately finished without an index to prevent your looking for a particular answer! The attitudes you need for good parental chastity education must be caught not taught. The attitudes your children need towards sexuality must be caught from you not taught by you!

Living the truth is not a matter of science or technology, not a matter of physiology, ethics, psychology, sociology, theology, history, etc., etc. It is simply a matter of living your life to the hilt with all the conviction you can bring to it, and allowing others to perceive the witness you are giving of the way you love with conviction or the lack of it. You will not succeed if you merely attempt what is expected of you without personal conviction. A perfunctory repetition of a "party line" whether religious, moral or patriotic will convince no one. You can only teach, in the area of chastity and modesty particularly, what you are truly convinced of, and which you have experienced and are still experiencing. That experience may include triumph and failure, satisfaction and remorse, virtue and sin, joy and sorrow, ease and struggle, honor and shame, courage and despair, love and hatred, devotion and abuse. A finally good life has often been full of sins or ambivalences, at best resolved, less good, muddled through, at least, repented and reversed.

Unfortunately, so much technical information is conveyed to young people today that is simply false or which suggests immoral or indifferently moral activity, that at times it is necessary to correct it with factual and moral truth drawn from science, or official religious teaching. This may suggest to parents that they consult some authority or official text, or even expect correct information from a trained teacher or counselor, priest, religious or lay person. But one must always ascertain the correct virtuous attitude of such a consultant.

Keep a sense of humor. Sexuality is too ridiculous to be treated pompously; too solemn, awesome, and frightening to be dismissed with mere matter of factness. It was of frightening import as to whose woman was Helen of Troy, whose beauty resided in the "face that launched a thousand ships." The great tragedies and epics, as well as the most delightful of comedies, center around the meaning of sexuality. *Hamlet* and *Othello* vie with *A Midsummer's Night Dream* and *The Taming of the Shrew* for our interest and attention. The contrast of tragedy and comedy is necessary for our sanity.

This book is deliberately repetitious. It will describe the same or similar suggestions in several different places or contexts. This is the way things happen with children. No child learns anything once and for all and on a single occasion. For that matter, no adult ever learns anything fully, completely, on a single occasion. An old adage say: "Repetition is the mother of learning." A weary father once sighed after "blowing his cork" unreasonably in the presence of his children: "I'll be so happy when they grow up realizing that I'm the one who (also) needs correction!"

CHAPTER I

The Right, Duty, And Privilege Of Sex Education By Parents

All education, whether formal or informal, is "rooted in the primary vocation of married couples to participate in God's creative activity" (*Familiaris Consortio* 36).

By begetting *in love* and *for love* a new person who has within himself or herself the vocation for growth and development, parents by that very fact take the task of helping that person effectively to live a fully human life. As the Second Vatican Council recalled, "Since parents have conferred life on their children, they have a most solemn obligation to educate their offspring. Hence, parents must be acknowledged as the *first* and *foremost* educators of their children. Their role as educators is so decisive that scarcely anything can compensate for their failure in it. For it devolves on parents to create a family atmosphere so animated with love and reverence for God and others that a well-rounded personal and social development will be fostered among the children. Hence, the family is the first school of those social virtues which every society needs (99).

The right and duty of parents to give education is *essential,* since it is connected with the transmission of human life; it is *original* and *primary* with regard to the educational role of others on account of the uniqueness of the loving relationship between parents and children; and it is *irreplaceable* and *inalienable* and therefore *incapable* of being entirely *delegated* to others or *usurped* by others.

... the most *basic element,* so basic that it sets the parameters of the educational role of parents, is *parental love,* which finds fulfillment in the task of education as it completes and perfects its service of life. As well as being a *source,* the parent's love is also the *animating principle* and therefore the *norm* inspiring and guiding all concrete educational activity, enriching it with the values of kindness, constancy, goodness, service, disinterestedness and self-sacrifice that are the most precious fruit of love (*Familiaris Consortio* 36, italics added).

Quite clearly the essential meaning of sexual intercourse is total mutual self-gift of husband and wife with deliberate risk or openness to whatever might happen of love and new human life. This is the paradigmatic sign or symbol-model of all other loves! Even God's love for man is a divine romance, a sort of divine-human marriage. Children should have been begotten of such mutual unconditional love, and if, because of human failure or sinfulness, a child happens "by accident" (or by deliberate pre-programming!) every possible remedial love must be employed to supply the fundamental *birthright* of every human being, to be sourced and supported in *disinterested* (risky!) love. Nothing can compensate fully for the lack of love as the *initiative*, or love as the *foundation* for the being and every form of education of the child. This is why the despised slave can sing poignantly "sometimes I feel like a motherless child." And why the only answer to the failed need is the overcompensating prophecy of Isaias: "Can a mother forget her nursing child, or show no compassion for the child of her womb? Even these may forget, I (God! Y-W-H!) will never forget you. See! I have inscribed you on the palms of my hands" (Isaiah 49:15-16).

Education of the child is *essential to* transmission of human life. Begetting is incomplete without education. Parental right, obligation and privilege is the origin of and primary to the role of any other teacher. Parental education cannot be replaced, and parents cannot hand it over entirely to others nor permit it to be forcibly taken over by others, no matter how professionally "qualified." Even bishops, priests and religious may not preempt true parental education. Parental love sets the extent of all education, is the source and animating principle of all education. The *norm* of good teaching by others is the love of the child's parents. Though minimum *schooling* can be legislated for the common good of society, in *education* parental love is everything.

> Education in love as self-giving is also the indispensable premise for parents called to give their children a clear and delicate sex education. Faced with a culture that largely reduces human sexuality to the level of something commonplace, since it interprets and lives it in a *reductive* and impoverished way by linking it solely with the body and with selfish *pleasure*, the educational service of parents must aim firmly at a training in the area of sex that is truly and fully

personal; for sexuality is an enrichment of the whole person — body, emotions, and soul — and it manifests its inmost meaning in leading the person to the gift of self in love.

Sex education, which is a basic right and duty of parents, must always be carried out under their *attentive guidance* whether at home or in educational centers *chosen* and *controlled* by them. In this regard the church reaffirms the law of subsidiarity, which the school is bound to observe when it cooperates in sex education, by entering into the same spirit that animates the parents.

In this contest education for chastity is absolutely essential, for it is a virtue that develops a person's authentic maturity and makes him or her capable of respecting and fostering the *"nuptial meaning* of the body. Indeed Christian parents, discerning the signs of God's call, will devote special attention and care to education in virginity or celibacy as the supreme form of that self-giving that constitutes the very meaning of human sexuality.

In view of the close links between the sexual dimension of the person and his or her ethical values, education must bring the children to a knowledge of and respect for the *moral norms* as the necessary and highly valuable guarantee for responsible personal growth in human sexuality.

For this reason the church is firmly opposed to an often widespread form of imparting sex information dissociated from *moral principles.* That would merely be an introduction to the experience of pleasure and a stimulus leading to the loss of serenity — while still in the years of innocence — by opening the way to vice (*Familiaris Consortio* 37, italics added).

According to this doctrine, sex education must be carried out by parents, and all others are but mere assistants. Schools, even Catholic schools, must cooperate with parents in this area, not vice versa!

Moral Principles

We are constantly reminded that sex education for Christians must never be divorced from moral principles. For that matter, it ought not be divorced from such principles for any sensible human being, Christian or not. Nor are the principles complex. They are really simple — and indeed, there is only one principle. Chastity is the moral principle which gives the simple meaning of sexual intercourse. Lovemaking is designed as the deepest mutual physical surrender of one man to one woman for a lifetime in mutual total self-giving with openness to whatever happens by way of result, whether deeper love or new-life or emptiness. The action means the same thing no matter what the partners mean! And it means the same thing even when they pervert it, abstain from it, open themselves to fertility with full awareness, or surrender to each other at times of infertility or even menopause. It means the same thing when they await the call of God for such surrender even for a lifetime in dedication to a vowed or situational celibacy or virginity!

When applied, this single principle looks complex. On this single principle, multiple sins are described and rejected as perverse rejections of the total nuptial meaning of the Body as a gift back to God in (truly) single blessedness *or* in marriage through one's husband or wife.

Masturbation is, sexually, like solitary drinking, "pigging out" or compulsive eating, as clearly also is the pursuit of pornography or obscenity. "Selfish use of partner as a sexual service station" or in some sort of bargain within marriage or outside it is a sort of prostitution, a (perhaps mutual) lust. Marital contraception is a mutual "lie in our bodies" as openness to new life, just as a verbal lie is speech that is "a lie in your teeth!" Sodomy (heterosexual) is the repulsive devotion to an opening of the body which is a death opening instead of a life opening. (Heterosexual) sado-masochism is the enactment of surrender, and demand for such surrender, to sheer overwhelming might instead of the loving request and avid surrender to the power of (mutual) authority which is exercised for the mutual good of the partners. Homosexual practice is devotion to the mirror image of the self, which inevitably rejects the life-giving meaning of sex, and which ends in either the utter emptiness of lesbianism or the disgusting devotion to death, defecation, and brutalities of male homosexuality. Why would anyone insist that sodomy is lovemaking, when we have spent so much effort on toilet training, and have reserved defecation to the privacy of the "*out*-house?" It cannot be without meaning that this practice of sodomy in marriage or in male homosexuality brings with it the sado-masochistic rectal lesions, repeated hepatitis, and the incurable AIDS (*Acquired* Immunological Deficiency Syndrome).

Obviously, there is no need for parents to describe all these perversions of the nuptial surrender of the body. A clear **in place** (in marriage) exclusive love-*meaning* will quite sufficiently indicate **out of place** (mutual) lust. An apparently crude "keep your panties up and your dress down!" within a loving family might well indicate the evil of lust and the positive celebration of Christian love-union in marriage! This is the reason St. Paul says that perversions of sex should not so much as be mentioned among Christians, and why he himself speaks of these perversions in circumlocutions, which quite clearly indicate his rejections but which are not vivid descriptions of the practices condemned (Eph 5:3-6).

A derived principle of **modesty** flows from Chastity. One *ought not* to start the sign activity which symbolizes, initiates and prepares for the mutual surrender of the nuptial *meaning* of the body, and one *ought* to willingly *mean* what these actions mean within the context of mutual and utter surrender in marriage. Mutual viewing, touch, kissing, open-mouth, tonguing, mutual exploration, is body-language reserved to the place where mutual total giving and receiving belong. As reserved to such a place (marital covenant and meaning) it is excluded absolutely elsewhere. "Do not stir up or awaken love until it is ready" (Song of Songs 2:7; 3:5; 8:4).

It is true that much physical affection before marriage can be a signal or promise, or mutual desire, for what is to happen after total commitment. Said a young lady to a counselor when her future husband complained that he could not get near her: "(Earthily) You want a ride? I'll give you the ride of your life. (Pointing to her ring finger) Put it there first!"

Parental Privilege

It is difficult to understand why parents might want others to give this formation to their children. Quite clearly, the culture in which we live does not believe these truths. It says that orgasm is desirable in itself, that it is a mere health entity to which each individual is entitled to experience as an option, as often as he or she wishes, alone or with any meaning he may desire and with as many partners of either sex (or even with animals) as they might choose. This is what the Pope means when he says that the modern approach is reductionist in that it makes of the meaning of nuptial surrender a "nothing but" a bodily experience of mere pleasure. Is he not right? Then how can you parents leave the formation of your children up to SIECUS (Sex Information and Education Council of the United

States), which controls all schooling on the topic and insists that unless the child has discovered sexual experience by himself, if we love the child we ought to make sure that he does.

This is one reason why, if at all possible, a mother should stay home as much as possible with her children, to be available for their formation as boys and girls, men or women, virgins and spouses, husbands or wives, fathers or mothers. Children need their spoken and unspoken questions answered when they need the answers, not when parents achieve "quality time." This is why I would like to recommend the statement of the mother who quit work in her late pregnancy: "Nobody else is going to form my child, answer his needs or questions. I an going to be there when he/she needs me." She recognized that there is pre-natal influence upon the child, and that how she and her husband/father accepted her pregnancy would influence that child, or, at least, how their resolution of their possible first ambivalences (Oh, **NO!**) will form the ultimate chastity of the child, as well as will the loving meaning given when the mother places her baby to her breast or tosses it on a pillow with a "bottle-caddy!" One wonders about the formation of child warehoused in a day-care center for ten hours a day at a cost roughly equivalent to the expense of kennel-boarding for a pet, or the daily city parking fee for a car. One wonders whether the care of the child is about equivalent to the care of the pet, or the car.

If the above paragraph evokes a feeling of guilt in the reader, please do not merely reject it with anger or denial. Resolve it by recognizing whether there is true justification for being away from the children, whether the child-care truly compensates for motherly care, and whether the decision is truly justified in the correct results. When one listens to the anxious questions a mother asks about professional or private child-care and day-care, it becomes more and more clear that the mother is looking for qualifications that only she herself can fill! All substitutional love must recognize that it is but a facsimile and (over) compensation for what should have been there in the first place. Adoptive parents, single parents, baby sitters, social workers, public welfare and agency personnel, day-care employees, etc., must attempt to **be** whatever parental person is missing in presence or function.

This in no way exempts the child from the need of paternal formation. A father is not merely the financial umbilical cord of life-support. His role of responsible concern, and personal attention to each and every child will teach his girls what to seek for in a husband-father and his boys the responsibility for and love for the possible wife-mother they will woo, wed and bed. The interaction of both will form the virility and femininity in their children necessary for either marriage or dedicated celibacy. The harm done to the chastity formation of children by the father who is absent physically or emotionally is incalculable.

Inevitability Of Parental Sex Education

Parents form their children in chastity or its lack no matter what they do! Whether they attempt to speak out, model correct nuptial body meaning, or fail to do so, whether they speak or remain silent, whether they succumb passively to the culture or the schooling of their children or fight and correct it, they are inevitably the final formers of their children. Though it might be that the culture and original sin will win out over parental Christian formation despite their best efforts, since "you can lead the horse to water but you cannot make him drink," parents are absolutely responsible for the lustful pursuits of their children if they abdicate all positive formation of their children.

Schooling is often too late and is as "scientific" as parental formation is "unscientific." Often parental example, positive, negative or omitted, "speaks so loudly that they cannot hear the intellectual truths taught in school. Preaching tends to be too brief, and indefinite (it is very difficult to be as concrete and earthy in the pulpit as parents can be in a one-on-one encounter. The religious education teachers (priest, sister, or lay man or woman), reach 25-30 pupils for only about 30 hours in a year! The most influential priest, religious, teacher or counselor in the world can, at most, be supportive or slightly corrective of parental example. No, parents must admit that in all the virtue formation of the child, and especially the chastity formation, "the (whole) buck stops here." By their presence or absence, by formation or its omission, by speech and action or their failure, parents are largely responsible for the chastity or unchastity, the modesty or immodesty of their children (granting always the final freedom of the child, and the cultural impact upon the fundamental weakness of will due to original sin).

This is not to say that the pope, bishops, priests, religious, teachers or counselors have nothing to say to parents by way of forming them to their duties, or to the community in correction of parental failure or even abuse of their authority. But the principle of subsidiarity is imperative here. This principle says that no duty should be performed by a more public authority if it can be and is being done by the private responsibility of individuals and families; that if the greater organization supplies what is lacking, it do so with the awareness that it is supplying only for a deprivation; that it protest that its supplement is essential temporary; and that as soon as possible, the role be returned to the original responsible actors. It is a notorious fact that all social tasks taken over by local or national public authority, tend to destroy individual responsibility, pauperizes, depersonalizes, and renders dependent the recipients of the services, and eventually refuses to return the function to the primary responsible persons! (E.g.; economic welfare, Aid To Dependent Children, Social Security, Juvenile and Family Courts, public schooling, health care insurance, bureaucratic controls of every kind, centralized school districts, even Catholic School Boards, public housing, care for the homeless, Soup Kitchens!)

Chapter II

Nuptial Meaning Of The Body

It is important for parents (and every human person, especially a Catholic Christian) to understand what John Paul II means by the "nuptial meaning of the body." He insists that the human being comes into the world as a body-soul person who is a unique gift from God with a unique call to surrender himself totally and completely to God, "You shall love the Lord your God with all your heart, and all you soul and with all your mind" (Mt 22:37; cf. Mk 12:30; Lk 10:27; in the Old Testament, Dt 6:5). "Whoever comes to me and does not hate his father and mother, his wife and children, brothers and sisters, yes, and even life itself, cannot be my disciple (Lk 14:26). (Cf. the weekly sermons of John Paul II from Sept. 1979 to July 4, 1984: *Original Unity of Man and Woman; Blessed Are the Pure of Heart; The Theology of Marriage and Celibacy;* St. Paul Editions, Boston MA 02130)

A nuptial or spousal gift is one that has been and will be given to no other than the beloved. Each human being (in Christian thought) is *uniquely* given by the creating hand of God into his own custody. A human person IS God's nuptial gift into the world, which is fresh, original, unique, inviolable, and never ever to be given again, nor will the identical gift be given to another. *Any* gift demands, as near as possible, an equivalent return of the gift. A *nuptial* gift can only be totally accepted from and wholly returned — to the giver and to no other. In the Holy Trinity the Father Utters Himself totally into the Son, the WORD. The WORD is totally receptive of the Uttering of the Father, and totally Echoes Divine Being back. You are mystified by this verbiage? Then mull over the mysterious wording of the Wedding Song: "A woman takes her life from man and gives it back again — there is Love." A nuptial gift can only be totally accepted. A nuptial gift must be gathered up and returned.

The human being enters into the material world, and his presence is signed, by being a body-person. In Christian thought the human body is not an appendage nor an instrument of a spirit. It is but the external

9

aspect, the visible material sign of the nuptial gift of human person into the world, and to the self. It must be returned, body and soul, unconditionally, holding nothing back, to the Creator. This is called the VOCATION of each and every person. A calling, a sounding into the world by God, which must be gathered up and returned to Him (and the Christian adds: "in Christ!").

This one gift of body and soul together which comes from the very hand of God with the cooperation of the mutual love-gift of husband and wife (called *pro*creation — i.e. an act evoking the creative act of God [cf. the meaning of sexual intercourse below]), must be returned in its entirety as a body-person to God. The Pearl of Great Price, for which the Christian must surrender all, is the acceptance of the total gift of self from God and its total return to Him. This, in turn, means that it is the task of the human person to "get himself all together" and wait till the expected moment to return this gift. This is the foundation of his duty to care for, develop and fulfill his potential, to grow to "the full stature of Jesus Christ" (Eph 4:13). His nuptial gift of self is his vocation as a Christian.

The call into being of the human person by God is an initial call to celibacy or virginity for all! A celibate (*Coelebs* in Latin) is one who achieves (or at least pursues) the fullness of what he truly is, singular and alone with a unique set of unshared potentials. Self-fulfillment is a celibate existence, and is given task of every human being as a nuptial given of God. But it is given to him to be totally returned. Self-fulfillment is self-possession in order to be returned utterly.

Celibacy or virginity is, therefore, the call of every human being, since celibacy means the ability to have oneself all together ready for a total self-gift. This gift can be given directly to God in a dedicated service for His Kingdom. It can be a situational celibacy when the opportunity for a gift to God through another person (marriage) does not present itself. It can be a temporary gathering together till the moment of gift to another in the name of God is presented. Finally, it is the "all together" of total self-gift in marital commitment.

Sexual Intercourse As A Sign Of Nuptial Gift And Return

At this point it is necessary to meditate on the inherent meaning of sexual intercourse. At first sight, as parents read this analysis, they will deny that they have ever heard such a thing. As they mull it over, however, they will agree that it is really a true presentation, but might object that it is an ideal beyond realization. But finally they will begin to admit that though they may never have heard it presented in such a way, this is really what they have always known the interpersonal action of sex is designed to mean, that they have always wanted to have it mean this, and that their own failures and disappointments have even proved the meaning!

They will even realize that despite their own possible practice of contraception in marriage, that marital contraception is a lie which they would rather not have their children discover in their parents, and which they really don't fully mean when they state the old mean-spirited adage: "and if you can't be good, be careful!" I know of no person, married or single, who is utterly unmoved by discovering contraceptives in the wallets of their children, or in the medicine cabinets of their parents. The movie "Prudence and the Pill" is hilarious precisely because contraceptive use is equally "out of place" for "mother," "daughter," or "maid." That each becomes pregnant while using pills from the same prescription, substituting placebos for those used, is clearly a "poetic justice" for all three.

Most human activities have whatever meaning the actor gives them. This most often depends entirely upon the intention of the actor. If I cook, I can cook because I am hungry, enjoy the kitchen, am interested in good nutrition, like sweets, want to gain weight, because I am a slave, need the money, am forced to by prison labor, because I want to invent a poison potion, or out of love for the people for whom I am cooking. Cooking does not have much meaning in itself.

But some human actions, besides being exerted for all sorts of motives as above, have some meanings built right into the activity so that it is difficult to have any meaning which would exclude the inherent meaning, or to engage in the activity without being lured into meaning what it means.

A Smile As Example Of Inherent Meaning

A smile is not just a combination of lips, facial muscles and eye movements. The grimace of an animal or even the puckering up of a newborn baby is not recognized as a smile. A smile is different from a frown, a scowl, a stare.

A smile is natural and spontaneous. We do not learn to smile as we learn to walk. Usually we do not first think of smiling and then do it. We just smile. A smile means the same thing in every culture, in every place in the world. And what does it mean? It means recognition, welcome, friendliness, love, joy, delight, content, amusement. But whatever it means it is hard to give it meaning outside itself, or at least being understood by everyone as what it is in itself.

A person who wants to smile for some ulterior purpose finds it difficult to do so, or if he succeeds, he seems to act perversely. Try to look into a mirror while imagining someone you dislike and say: "I'm smiling at you, you big baboon!" You will see a terrible grimace as you force the same muscles used in a smile to pretend to smile. Or smile while you are betraying a friend, and you will note a perverse gleam which mocks the benevolence of a smile as you destroy him.

Strangely too, if you are suddenly tricked into smiling, your whole mood will change. Notice how often lovers who have become angry with each other will drop the whole dispute, when one can get the other to even begin a smile!

A Kiss

Another kind of activity which has meaning woven right into it is kissing. It has been said that Eskimos express love by rubbing noses, and that they do not know what a kiss means. I would like to suggest that any Eskimo man or maid would immediately know what a kiss meant if you could get him or her to pucker up and experience a kiss! A kiss "says": "Taste and see that my beloved is sweet" (cf. Ps 33:9)! A kiss shares the very life breath of the lovers. It opens the being of the lover to the beloved and vice versa.

It is hard to fake a kiss. The beloved knows immediately if a kiss is perfunctory, or worse, a betrayal. Indeed, to use the externals of a kiss to betray is a most perverse act. Mafia members use the kiss deliberately as a "kiss-off" before the execution of a member who is considered guilty of betrayal. When Jesus was betrayed by Judas with a kiss, He did not ask whether Judas intended to betray Him. He did not say: "Are you betraying me who did so much for you?" He said: "Judas do you betray the Son of Man with a kiss?!" "Are you delivering me to execution with **the** sign which means love, concern, devotion?"

But equally often, a kiss that starts out as merely perfunctory, a mere dutiful response to an advance, a casual contact, allures the one who kisses to mean what it means with more and more intensity, even against his will, and to evoke a similar response from an apparently uninterested partner.

Sexual Intercourse

Sexual Intercourse is one human activity which has the deepest of inherent meanings. It is possible to engage in this activity with outside intentions — of escape from boredom, to scratch the itch of passion, to please an ardent seducer, to boast of a conquest, to win esteem when one feels worthless, even to make money — but that is not what the action means in itself. Notice that we avoid the cold scientific terms for this activity. Intercourse is the ebb and flow (coursing) of something (fluid, affection, communication, life) between two persons; coition means a mere coming together; coupling or copulation is mere connection followed by disconnection, uncoupling. Mating is what we use for animals in heat. And, of course, the four-letter words are brutal references to piercing, hurting, rejection, or the in-heat activities of rutting animals ("bang," "screw," "filly," "stud," — to use only the least repulsive!). When a man and a woman can use only mechanical or animal words for their love-union they have reduced each other to non-persons, to things or mere animals, and have perverted the meaning of sexual intimacy. We prefer words like lovemaking, being intimate with. To "make-love" means to make love present in the bodily sign of "two-in-one." To "be intimate with" means to mutually explore the innermost depths of the lovers as persons.

Lovemaking

What is sexual union between human being designed to mean? First, love-union is the only activity the author knows which takes two people, one a man and the other a woman, to mean what it is designed to mean. Conversation is a somewhat similar activity, but in conversation one speaks while the other listens and then reverses the activity. In love-union

two people mean, or are invited to mean, one reality: "two-in-one-flesh."
This two-in-one-ness is not mere bodily connection. The word "flesh"
here means a human person, body and soul. To become two-in-one means
to experience the other's body-person as I feel my own. When Adam sang
the first love poem in the Bible: "This now is bone of my bone, flesh of
my flesh" he was singing the same sort of song we sing today, when we
sing "Heart of my Heart," and "I've got you under my skin." And when
the Bible concludes "Therefore a man leaves his father and mother and
clings to his wife and they become one flesh" (Gn 2:24), it means that this
union signs and means that these two are as inseparable as a head is from
the rest of a human body. To lose the partner is more than the loss of a
limb, it is to lose one's own self! This is why spouses joke about "my
better half." "Making love" asks the couple to mean what it means —
being one person — and the activity tends to progressively make them
one whether they mean it or not!

A deeper look into the activity of love-union reveals that a man and a
woman are asked to act out the deepest of love meaning. I do not have a
body as a writer has a fountain pen or a typewriter. I **am** my body. Or
better, I — body-self — exist. Love union does not mean copulation. That
is merely the coupling of active and receptive connectors. The man is
invited to focus his whole person on the loveliness of his bride and to
penetrate into the deepest recesses of her being. He is asked to say: "I in-
you me," that is, "I place my entire being within you." On her side the
wife is asked to accept her husband's entire substance into her very being.
She tries to say: "I in-me you," that is, "I carry your entire person within
mine; I accept your centering into the center of my person!"

Baby Making

To understand this further make a comparison with a woman who is
pregnant. I think there may be many undesired pregnancies (experience of
being gravid) but hardly ever a truly unwanted baby. Especially if a
mother comes to understand that during pregnancy that she has been
entirely surrounding another body-person with her body-person. She has
experienced what love is — which is to discover another self as central to
her own self as she is! And if she is lucky enough to have been able to
deliver her baby while conscious of what she is doing, she will have
experienced the uttering of a brand new Word, a new Meaning, an origi-

nal Edition, never before heard, and never to be repeated. This is why she wants a unique name for her baby. But this experience is just an elaboration of her experience of her husband-lover which brought it to be. The baby is "two-in-one-flesh" just as the lovers are. Just as the lovers are two distinct persons but become one person which is distinct from the both of them (they say: "this is bigger than the both of us together!"), so the baby is at once both of them — and neither of them! More important than anything in the world. This is why we say that a baby was a gleam in his daddy's eye in their love, and why simple country people used to say that love was "getting a baby in the eye of the beloved." Finally, that is what is meant in the Hawaiian love song to a newborn child:

> Sweet Leilani, heavenly flower
> Nature fashioned roses wet with dew.
> And then she laid them in a bower.
> That was the start of you.
>
> Sweet Leilani, heavenly flower.
> I dreamed of paradise for two.
> Your are my paradise completed.
> You are my dream come true.

Total Self-Gift

But sexual union is designed to mean still more. If the male is expected to center all his being upon the person of the beloved, and she is expected to take all of him into her person, then the action attempts to say: "All that I am, all I have ever been, all I ever will be I give to you" and "All that you are, have been, or ever will be, I accept totally and absolutely from you." An old song says: "All of me, why not take all of me?" But if this is to be true then the act ought to protest that no one else has ever had any part of this gift before! The act asks the actors to say: "No one has ever gone this way with me before, and no one but you will ever go this way again." This is why lovers are always jealous if they suspect that any other has had access to the body person of the lover or beloved, and why they would rather not know of any past love affairs. A Country and Western song asks: "How many hearts have you broken? I wonder, I wonder, I wonder — **but I really don't want to know.**"

Faithful

If the sexual act surrenders not only the past and the present, but also the future, then it asks the lovers to be faithful to each other. How long? Forever. There are no meaningful love songs which celebrate temporary unions. We sing only: "Forever and ever"; "Till the end of time"; "I'll love you till the twelfth of never, and that's a long, long time." Diamonds are **not** a girl's best friend! This is the poignant song of a courtesan who cannot expect fidelity.

"No Strings" Love

The mutual surrender of sexual union is called the marital or conjugal act. It is unconditional. It does not say: "I love you so long as you are beautiful. I love you when you have money. I love you only when you are nice to me. I give you only part of myself. I hold my freedom from you. No strings! I don't want you to make me pregnant. I love you so long as you don't get pregnant. I love you till I fall in love with someone else!" It does say: "I'll always love you, even when you are less than nice, indeed when you are hateful. More, because you might be unlovely I will make you loving and lovable by my love!" No strings. Unconditional surrender of each to the other.

Modesty

This unconditional mutual surrender of past, present and future is the real reason for both modesty and nudity between lovers. Modesty guards the secret of one's own private personhood from casual invasion. Just as I do not want anyone to read my personal letters, listen in on my phone calls, read my diary, and want to respect the privacy of others by refusing to pry, eavesdrop, break and enter, or even to demand confidences, so modesty of dress protects one's sexual secret from anyone but the committed lover! Modesty of eyes refuses to invade the secret of anyone but the beloved, and that only upon invitation, mutual and total surrender, with awe and reverence for the holiness and inviolability of sexual personhood — which clearly reserves this to marriage. It is incredible that promoters of absolutely liberal choice use a "right to privacy" to choose to kill an unborn child while opening their bodies to all viewers and all comers and boast of "letting it all hang out."

On the other hand, nudity, however hesitant, fearful, awe inducing, shy, is the uniform of mutual surrender. Between committed spouses, it is a statement: "I give you all of myself, I hold nothing back. I do not hide behind convention, dress, make-up, pretense. I an vulnerable to you in all my failures, helplessnesses, less than attractive features. We are mutually vulnerable to pregnancy, its 'labor' and responsibilities."

At first, nudity may tend to mere sexual stimulus at the physical beauty or virility of the beloved. Later, the revelation of all the body's weariness in service of the lover-beloved and children will be but an ever more impressive sign of total mutual surrender. As life traces its wear and tear on the bodies of lovers, and their good and evil choices make their permanent marks, the mutual acceptance and surrender becomes more and more precious and is clearly manifest in the mutual acceptance of each other's bodily reality. A man who finds his wife's ungainly body, pregnant with his very own child, repulsive to him, does not have the faintest idea of what mutual love means! Nor does the wife find her weary and tiring husband and father less romantic because he no longer looks like a knight in shining armor.

Chastity

The same concept of total unconditional giving and receiving which is marital love lies at the basis of the beautiful reality of chastity. Chastity is a language of the body-person which says: "No one but my beloved has gone this way before and no one but he will ever go this way again." Every man would prefer his wife to be a virgin, and every woman would prefer to surrender her sexual personhood to her husband untouched, unsullied in having been passed through many exploratory hands or temporary liaisons. Unfortunately, few women seem to demand virginity of experiencing from their future husbands; fewer men see any desirability in being sexually celibate till they consummate their marriages. Indeed, the male so boasts his machismo — his sexual prowess in seducing, overcoming and impregnating females, that he even succumbs to a negative hypocrisy, and pretends experiences which he has hardly even read about! Yet often enough, after multiple partners, he demands virginity of a woman he wants as a wife. This is (however unconscious) the mutual recognition of the spousal or nuptial meaning of the body.

Failure

More unfortunately, human nature is so weak and the sexual drive so mysteriously strong that many of us do not arrive at maturity with an achieved sexual integrity; we do not have our sexual "act together", our "heads on straight" in this area. Mercifully, though once virginity is lost it is lost forever, there is the possibility of sorrow, a reversal of direction, and forgiveness. A kind of secondary virginity.

Such forgiveness must be threefold. One who has failed in chastity must first forgive himself when he finds himself a failure and wishes to reverse his field. Then he must seek forgiveness of the one whom he has harmed (his future spouse or present partner). This is why lovers almost always are driven to confess past sexual failures to the beloved — a confession that is not always wise! (It might be wiser to presume the forgiveness than to hurt by detailing the infidelity). Finally, he must approach the God who has designed the mysterious meaning of sex. Of these three the only certain forgiveness will come from God (who antecedently is willing to forgive and redeem if only the sinner is willing to repent, confess), who is far more forgiving than a partner or even a remorseful self. "Remorse" means a bitter "biting back" at the thought of shameful failure. Often remorseful (not sorrowful!) sinners make their own "hell" by wallowing in despising themselves. But if God can forgive a person he must learn to forgive himself. The Bible is full examples in which God forgives sexual unchastity upon sorrow. David's adultery with Bethsheba and murder of her husband is a case in point. David's beautiful Song for Forgiveness is full of sorrow but confidence in God's forgiveness which enabled him to move on (Psalm 51).

The God of the Hebrews saw the entire nation as His repeatedly adulterous wife, whom He forgave again and again when she returned to Him. Jesus forgave the woman actually taken in the act of adultery while saying to her: "Nor do I condemn you. You may go. But from now on, avoid this sin" (Jn 8:11). He insisted that no reason whatever permitted divorce and remarriage when a partner failed to please. "Therefore, let no man separate what God has joined" (Mt 19:6).

Perversity

Like using a smile to deceive and a kiss to betray, the enactment of sex while refusing to mean what it means is perverse. Love union is the mutual surrender of one man to one woman with openness to a child for a lifetime. Love is unconditional surrender. Love can never be careful or conditional, can never reject involvement, refuse or reverse consequences. A boy too young to marry who insists on being paid for a date with sexual intimacy is as destructive of himself and the girl as a Mafia member betraying with a kiss! A girl who seduces a date to prove her desirability, to reassure herself that she is feminine and lovable, or to hold on to a relationship she suspects cannot last, misuses her body to snare the boy in an involvement he cannot sustain. He acts and demands a response which says eternal surrender with utter abandon, but he perverts it my making it a monetary uninvolved encounter. She tries to use the sexual act as a mere means to hold him to support her immaturity, her need for affection. Real love is self-surrender not self-service. The "guy" who slips the girl a few hundred dollars for an abortion, and walks away from her without responsibility, has been a liar in his loins.

Like the smile and the kiss, sexual intercourse also betrays the partner to mean what they as yet do not mean, and can not yet mean. A boy and a girl might merely want to express affection, or to discover what the sexual experience might be like. They might protest that there are to be "no strings," that there is no thought of permanence or of marriage. All the protests in the world will not prevent them from getting "hung up" on each other! Immediately upon sexual interaction, they both become intensely involved with each other. (The word "involve" means "rolled up into": surely coitus **is** involvement!). They are immediately jealous of any contact with any third person of the same peer group, or even of the influence or love of parents. They fiercely demand a loyalty as intense as any that might be expected of a husband and wife committed to each other by solemn vows before God. They become even more suspicious of the partner's "infidelity" because they both know that this one is *not* a commitment and that other contacts are equally non-committal. The agony of insecurity which flows from an act which "says" faithful commitment while not having the certainty of a marriage contract or covenant is full of fear and terror at the inevitability of disaster. The tragedy of heartbreak when it is all over has been the theme of half the love songs in the world — which are known as Blues' Songs. "Baby, oh baby, oh baby, you said you'd come again this way again — **maybe** — *I* love you true."

Nor can the sexual act mean less than an openness to conception. A couple, in or out of marriage, who insist on donning a contraceptive, or inserting contraceptive armor or chemicals are acting out a lie. Lovemaking and baby making are one and the same identical activity. The baby making act invites the couple to open themselves totally to each other. A man gives himself, and hence his virility, his seed and his fertility to his beloved. He gives her the substance of his body, and he *is* that substance! A woman surrenders her total femininity to him, and hence her potential as a mother. That is an essential part of her as a woman. She too *is* totally her body. It is no accident to the procreative meaning of sexual love that a woman is more desirous of bodily affection when she is ovulating! When a couple use contraceptives they are contradicting themselves. He puts his substance in a garbage bag, or she armors herself against him, uses chemical warfare to defend herself against him. Or she makes of herself a spayed human being, or a rejector of his child for a longer or shorter time (pill, IUD), a (excuse!) bag for his effluvia.

It is difficult to lie since our whole bodies protest when we try lying. This is why the lie detector works, and why we cry: "You lie in your teeth! (meaning that your very teeth are blocking your words)" when we catch someone. So our bodies protest when we attempt to use contraceptives. The abandon of lovemaking is impatient with the calculated delay needed to don or insert the contraceptive. One is uncomfortable with the premeditated calculation and repeated choices necessary to stay on the pill every day, or to wear or carry a contraceptive. The decision to be "always ready" accepts that the boy or girl is "that kind" of a person. Love cannot be calculating, fearful, rejective, conditioned upon no "unwanted" outcome, or only antecedently chosen results. Love is essentially total risk!

Unwanted Pregnancy?

Like the smile and kiss that "trick" an angry lover to respond with a smile and to return the kiss with more and more response-ability, so a baby making act draws the couple to open themselves to pregnancy.

Contraceptives do not work very well. It is hard to trap, bloc, immobilize or kill 200 million+ sperm in an ejaculation, when the facilitating conditions for their motility are present at ovulation. The search and destroy mission of modern contraception is notably a failure. Note that back-up is advised — a diaphragm *with* a spermicide. (Kill! Kill! Kill!) Wherever sex education is initiated with concentration on how people act sexually and how to avoid conception, unanticipated pregnancies increase in direct proportion to the instruction and the availability of the contraceptives. Discussions of methods of sexual release without discussing the meaning quite naturally stimulate the students to explore sexual release to find "what it's all about." It is not always possible, and it turns out to be "not nice to fool Mother Nature." It is usually argued that since ours is a sex-saturated culture, and young and old people are going to get into sexual activities anyway, the only way to avoid a surprise pregnancy is to increase the knowledge and availability of contraceptives. It is curious that no one ever questions that with every increase of availability, there is an increase of premarital and extramarital pregnancies, and an increase in the demand for more and more easily available abortion. The Gutmacher Institute (of Planned Parenthood) admits that the only reason for abortion is backup for contraceptive failure. If the human person is unique and irrepeatable, every conception and every person *must be* a surprise! Uniqueness cannot be planned, programmed, anticipated, conditioned.

But contracep*tives* do not fail as much as contracep*tors* do! Physicians who prescribe medicine speak of "method failures" and "patient failures." These terms describe medicines which fail, and patients who fail to take the medicine! It would seem that the mechanics and instrumentation of contraception do not always work, but that more often people do not "work" them. Since when is a healthy woman a "patient" for whom a remedy for fertility must be prescribed? This whole idea makes pregnancy a disease, and the sperm of her lover an infectious bacteria to be defended against, a venereal disease not really different from gonorrhea or herpes!

Many young people are quite knowledgeable about contraceptives and their availability, yet they do not even think of using them. Why? I often wonder whether they wish to discover the meaning of sex in all its amplitude before they start to prevent meaning. After they have started sexually and (perhaps) panicked at a missed period and have gone for a pregnancy test which turned out negative, they do use contraceptives more often, but then "forget" them from time to time (usually at ovulation?). Why? Even an act of omission has a reason, though perhaps an unconscious one. Pregnancy is a proof of maturity, a declaration of independence from family, a method of luring into marriage, the provision of someone whom I cannot help loving, or who cannot help loving me. Making a baby is a very creative experience when one is prevented from other creativity by immaturity, lack of other skills, artistic ability, complete education. It is a very inexperienced counselor who does not ask himself, when a young or old couple come in with a problem pregnancy or the suspicion of one: "Why did he/she *want* to make/be pregnant?"

The logic of Planned Parenthood Federation of America seems irrefutable: In a sexually stimulative culture, where all citizens are expected to be sexually active in all possible ways, unanticipated pregnancies should be prevented by effective contraceptives, and accidents removed by abortions. "Every child (ought to be permitted to exist only if he is antecedently) a wanted child!" "Children (can be permitted to **be** only) by Choice not be Chance!" Strangely, this logic does not work the desired results. We now have more premarital and extramarital pregnancies, more children born to unwed women, more teenage marriages, more abortion remedies and more marital breakups than ever in the history of the world. More of the same remedy only seems to make matters worse, so something must be wrong.

The logic of the truth of sex is quite different. Sex means that two people, one a man and the other a woman, are invited to mean a total mutual gift of virility and femininity to each other with openness in utter unconditional surrender to whatever happens of life and love. If, for any reason, the two cannot or ought not to mean what sex means (whether because of immaturity, health, finances, psychic or social reasons), they ought not to "say" what sex says at this time. It is not true that sexual drive is insurmountable. A compulsive user of sex is not a giver but a taker. Sex is surely less demanding than the instinct of self-preservation, yet even here we have thousands of records of those who have risked their own lives out of love for others. We call some heroes. But we expect and take for granted this kind of risk in our police, fireman, doctors, lifeguards, and even our mothers and fathers. It would be a strange man who would insist upon "lovin" his wife when she had a heart condition and could die in his arms. It must be a strange young man who with a date will argue: "If you loved me you would, and if you won't, you have a sexual hangup!" Or even: "What's your problem — you're on the pill, aren't you?"

Abstinence

It should be quite obvious that for all truly human activity which is freely initiated, abstinence is as necessary as use. In communication, silence is as important as speech. The compulsive babbler gets "turned off." In the words of the song: "Don't speak of love, show me! **Now!**" The compulsive eater is piggish and repulsive. Only one who can fast, can feast! Now that we have rediscovered the probable moments of fertility in the married couple, a fertility awareness celebrated long before we knew anything about biology by pre-Christian Jews and even by David and Bethsheba in their criminal and murderous adultery, it is quite clear that there is "A time to embrace and a time to refrain from embracing. . . A time to keep silence, and a time to speak. . . ." (Eccl 3:5). (Cf. Rabbi Normal Lamm: *A Hedge of Roses.*)

Scriptural Meaning of Sexual Intercourse

Judaeo-Christian tradition has a rich awareness of the meaning of sexual intercourse, which transcends and completes the meaning which is clearly observable by any thoughtful person. It is important to realize that religion does not supplant the perception of common sense, but that it more fully unfolds and fulfills it.

The earliest books of the Old Testament clearly analyze the meaning of sexuality. Adam saw that sex was meant to make two persons, a man and a woman, to be as near as possible a single person. This is the reason lovers speak of: "My other self" or even "my better half." Adam said:

> This at last is bone of my bones and flesh of my flesh; this one shall be called Woman, for out of Man this one was taken. Therefore a man leaves father and mother and clings to his wife, and they become one flesh. And the man and his wife were both naked and were not ashamed.

Notice that there is a special play on words here. In Hebrew the word for man is "ish" and the word for woman is "ishah." This is the same as calling the woman "sweetheart" or "heart of my heart." The word *woman* (wo = out of, man = earthy) really means that she is as central to him as he is to himself!

But there is also a blessing upon this union:

> So God created humankind in his own image, in the image of God he created them. Male and female he created them. And God blessed them and God said to them, "Be fruitful and multiply and fill the earth and subdue it; and have dominion over the fish of the sea and

over the birds of the air and over every living thing that move upon the earth (Gn 1:27-28).

The original Hebrew has a deeper meaning here. The blessing means: "Make love (or open your love to children) and multiply. . . Extend human beings throughout the earth and bring it under your wise and prudent control."

Jesus makes it quite explicit that the description of "two in one flesh" is not merely a metaphor, symbol, sign or ideal but a true existential or ontological reality. In His "argument" that divorce is not possible, He adds: "Therefore what God has joined together, let no one separate" (Mt 19:6). He dismisses all arguments for exceptions in hardship cases. When His disciples argue that it would be better not to marry than to risk an unhappy union — He agrees! He says equivalently, if unconditional love is not what you want in marriage, do not marry!

St. Paul makes it clear that unchastity is sinful by insisting that lustful action is a sin against one's own body-person and also against the Body of Christ. He clearly states that Christian married couples, in their love union, should "glorify God in your body." (Read the whole section in 1 Cor 6:15-20.)

Finally, St. Paul makes clear that total mutual commitment of man and woman in Christian marriage is a reliving and a making present again of the union of Christ and His Church. Christian husband and wife are to love each other and to express this love in the name and place of Jesus Christ as Head and Jesus Christ as His Body — the Church which is His Mystical but Real Body. (Cf. Eph 5: 21-33; for an elaboration of the celebration of Christian sexual love, cf. Henry V. Sattler, *Sex Is Alive And Well And Flourishing Among Christians,* Anastasia Press, Stafford VA 22554, 1979, Chapter 6).

Chapter III

Process Of Sex Education In The Home

If sex is the quality of masculinity or femininity in a person, then sex education should be the provision of formation and information for a boy to reach maturity as a man and a girl to reach maturity as a woman. This is chastity education, since it implies a norm of masculine and feminine roles in, or in view of, marriage and family, whether an individual marries or lives as a celibate or virgin.

If this can be called sex education, it seems logical to begin wherever the necessity for information and attitudinal formation begins to be needed in the lifetime of a growing person. In days gone by, very little, if any, *formal* (universal *schooling* is a relatively recent phenomenon!) information was given and individuals learned by experimentation and a set of modeled attitudes suggesting very indirectly (but effectively!) that genital sex activity belonged only in marriage with orientation to children, and that fatherhood and motherhood was the paradigm or model of all sexual maturity. There is really very little record of how sexual information or attitudes were taught or formed in days gone by. How people learned about sexual, bodily, character, and role differences, menstruation and seminal emission, the interaction of boy and girl, man and woman, husband and wife, conception and childbirth, mother and father, parent and child, was absorbed within the family and in the community but often not recorded. A largely illiterate population was neither written *for* nor *about!*

As more frequently used today, particularly in public school education, "sex education" indicates a classroom study of the ways in which men and women achieve orgasm alone or with a partner, the options open to them, the results which might happen in terms of psychic "hang-ups, venereal disease or pregnancy and the possibilities of institutionalizing or at least socializing various orgasmic life-styles. This is *sexology,* a dubiously "modern" science less than a century old, beginning with Havelock Ellis! Hardly a home-taught discipline!

When sex education first became a public or social question, it almost immediately became an education in sexology, and not a matter of role identification. It was first directed to the married who were taught techniques of sexual variation (e.g., Van de Velde, *Ideal Marriage*) and it was followed by methods of avoiding pregnancy necessary if sexual release is to be achieved as often as one wills without unprogrammed outcome. When someone noted that it might be too late to learn these facts and skills in marriage, it was suggested that this should be involved in preparation for marriage, a new kind of formal education never provided before. Families with a number of children born at home knew quite well about love, pregnancy, childbirth, and the role of parents, children and siblings.

When the same kind of pregnancy prevention became generally available, there was no reason why sexual release should be reserved to marriage, and the *sexual revolution* was initiated. At present, one is looked at with disbelief if he remarks that he holds that sex belongs only in marriage with openness to whatever happens. And, of course, official Catholic teaching on this topic is rejected by most in their belief, and ignored even more in practice. Even Catholics do not markedly differ from their non-believing friends in their practice of pre and extramarital sex, contraception, abortion, divorce — or even infanticide.

Again, since this knowledge was avidly absorbed by the unmarried as well as the married, the more rapid spread of venereal diseases and the spectre of unwanted premarital as well as marital pregnancy demanded greater information and techniques both to achieve orgasm and to avoid all the outcomes thereof, including the stigmas of social disapproval for any marital disintegration of orgasm alone or among consenting adults ("adult" for sexual purposes meaning the moment of orgasmic potential and desire — adolescence: 10 to 13 for a girl; 14-15 for a boy).

Logically, genital activity alone and with others began to be accepted and then anticipated on ever lower and lower age levels. It was *logically* argued that, if individuals were to become sexually active at any particular age, they ought to be instructed on what the outcomes of their sexual activity might be and how to avoid what might be undesired. With the acceptance of sexual activity as soon as the child was capable, since the 1920's it has become miniminally argued that whenever a child could possibly experience orgasm and intromission, he or she ought to be provided with the information about how this is achieved, what it does and very specifically the undesirability of *any* outcome at such an early age, romantic involvement, commitment (marriage or equivalent), pregnancy or STD's. (Sexually Transmitted Diseases — Note that this term has been introduced as a substitute for what were once called venereal diseases, since the latter term implied some sinful cause. The new term implies morally insignificant cause, like sneezing in public as a source of viral infection.)

In all this, sex education became more and more focused upon tumescence and orgasm, functional coitus, the pleasurable and psychological meanings of such activity, the outcomes of venereal disease, the probability of pregnancy which was almost always considered undesirable, even in marriage, or desirable *only* when arbitrarily and antecedently chosen. Sexual activity has now been expected and inculcated in children not only at puberty but at ever earlier years. We therefore have sex education programs from kindergarten to grade 12 and further information on the college level. It has even been indicated by leaders in SIECUS, (Sex Information and Education Council of U.S.) that preschool children should be informed about orgasm and attitudinalized favorable towards it at an even earlier age: "Sex is so good and important a part of life that if children don't happen to discover sexual enjoyment for themselves, if we really like them, we will make sure that they do" ("Parents Wary of Suppressing Sexuality in Children," in *New York Times,* May 17, 1983)!

If an awareness of sexualness and sexuality must be *taught,* a formal program must be begun, no later than birth. If however, sexualness and sexuality are aspects of becoming a person which are *caught,* then we must begin with models of mature adults in marriage, virginity and celibacy. We must make children aware of what a happily successful sexual human man and woman might approximately look like in his or her perfection. A child can not really be taught truthfulness when he begins to speak. Nor will it help to study the physiology of speech. Truthfulness must be exemplified before this in those around him. He cannot be instructed in good music, nor learn much about it from studying sound or the physiology of hearing. He must hear it in his environment. He cannot be told about the joys of sexual maturity in marriage or celibacy, he must observe such happy maturity in models.

This does not preclude some formal instruction, philosophical and theological research, or biological and psychological information. It merely makes all of these things satisfactory to interiorization by imitation, however vaguely understood. The implication of our present sexual education craze is that no adult could possibly or fully understand either sexualness or sexuality or achieve its satisfactory maturity without a graduate degree in sexology (which is the study of how human beings achieve orgastic release). For all less well schooled people, sexology must be simplified and taught in every grade level of schooling down to preschool picture books. A recent survey of sexual knowledge insists that knowledge about the frequency of premarital coitus and the frequency of homosexual orgasm is necessary for healthy sexual adjustment!

What then is the goal of sex-education? What is the picture of its achievement? If the goal of being a man and woman is the achievement of every variety of sexual release with the elimination of every unanticipated and unprogrammed outcome, the modern sex education program in the school system should be implemented and parents and religion should be excluded from the process! They do not have the necessary "science" of sexology. But if the goal is successful and contented celibacy or family life, then our present school system is the worst possible since it triggers, encourages, and facilitates the pursuit of the greatest possible number of orgasms, and the greatest variety and intensities of orgastic experience. It must, since it teaches no control of activity, teach control and reversal of sexual consequences (hygiene for V.D., contraception, abortion, infanticide, separation, divorce, emotional therapy for guilt, insecurity, hatreds, jealousies — all the disasters over which we shed vicarious tears as we watch the "soaps" on TV).

The Fullness Of Sexualness And Sexuality

Christian sexual formation (or chastity education) must begin with the parents. Parents must have a clear idea of what being a man, and being a woman, and what sexual lovemaking might truly mean even if they have not achieved it in practice. Further, no matter how many their failures, they must both have some awareness of the value of virginity and celibacy both in its dedication to God and its dedication to partner by virginal arrival to the marriage union. This is chastity.

Six months before her wedding, Marian spoke to Jack, "Look, I want the joy of celebrating our wedding night with a "never before" virginal gift of myself to you and hopefully a receiving from you your virginal gift. But it's getting harder and harder for me to resist your importunity and my own passionate and romantic love for you. I hereby hand myself and my body over to you, surrendering it to you so that you will bring it to the marital bed a virgin body. You are going to be responsible for making love to me, to impregnate me, and to care for me during my pregnancies, and to support me and the children as they grow, as well as to educate them. Your responsibility for me and them starts now!" Jack protested that that was not fair, that she too had the obligation to help *him* arrive virginally to the marriage bed. Marian agreed that she should not be seductive nor excessively amorous during the remaining time of engagement, but that she would no longer feel obligated to say "No" in emphatic tones, nor to fend off each and every advance. Whether they succeeded or failed in reaching their marriage sexually inviolate, I do not know. I know that I respect their concern and mutual responsibility for action or restraint.

In similar fashion, each parent must strive to continually interiorize a total pattern of masculinity or femininity eventuating in fatherhood or motherhood. This does not mean the attempt to approximate some stereotype of virility or femininity. It means that each person, from observation, must try to approximate multiple examples of true virility or femininity because each will have to try to exemplify for the growing boy or girl, the points of identification which will provide the discovery of sexual identity in the child. It is important that a man enjoy being virile. That he accepts the challenge of initiative, positive agressivity, leadership and responsibility for his own actions and for the security, safety, happiness, and indeed, the maturation of each and every member of his family. With President Truman, a husband and father must have as his motto "the buck stops here". This applies equally to the sexual initiative which *begins* his "matrimony" the state of making a mother. (Matrimony — from the Latin "matri" — towards a mother, "munus" — official function). As well as the responsibility for the welfare of the woman and children he initiates into marriage (the way of a man with a maid) and family life.

In days gone by, a father was responsible for the virginity of his daughter and, therefore, presented her *veiled* to her husband at her wedding. Unfortunately the macho image of muscle flexing and sexual prowess of the past did not seem to provide the model of male celibacy as responsibility for his son, and often a father was hardly a model of spousal integrity for his sons entering marriage. But this has always been a position of Christianity from the day that St. Paul clearly said that a male did not have the ownership of his own body, but his wife did, and the woman did not have the ownership of her own body, but her husband did (1 Cor 7:4). Ownership does not mean possessiveness here, but responsibility for welfare! Care! Answerableness!

On her side a wife and mother ought early to have interiorized the song "I enjoy being a girl." This means coming to terms with her bodily differences from the male, her relative lack of strengths and competitive spirit, the ebb and flow of mood-inducing hormones from the moment of puberty, the regular reminder of fertility in bodily changes accompanying ovulation and the sloughing off baby nourishment from the lining of her uterus (cf. Ingrid Trobisch, *The Joy of Being a Woman and What a Man Can Do,* Harper and Row, 1975).

A wife must also adjust to a fundamental helplessness. When the final chips are down and her passion of love fully aroused, she is helpless in her surrender to conjugal union, to a pregnancy which might be less than desirable at any given moment, and the fact that her baby takes over the room in her body with utmost arrogance and makes her more and more gravid — weighty and *important* indeed — but *weighed down!*

She too, having attempted with whatever success or failure to reach her marriage bed virginally, must exemplify the modesty and reserve for her girls and boys which will draw the boys to seek and be virginal partners and the girls to look forward to the surrender, whether to God directly in consecrated virginity, or to sacramentally present herself to Christ in husband! This will demand the exemplification of modesty within the home and between husband and wife within reason.

Adam and Eve were naked and unashamed before original sin because there was no possibility of sexual appetite suddenly stirring before they had chosen to approach each other in loving surrender. Nevertheless, Saint Thomas Aquinas teaches that since their beings would have been totally at the service of their free will, not in rebellion against it, their love expression before the fall must have been all the more intensely enjoyable! Only after the fall did they discover sexual concupiscence (which is not appetite, but appetite *for itself* — lust!) and find it necessary to clothe themselves against sudden, meaningless and undesirable sexual appetite. John Paul II in his discussion of the Spousal Meaning of the Body, suggests that Christian husband and wife are attempting, over a long period of living together, to achieve that spousal surrender which does not seek the partner in mere lust or mutual use and service, but in concern totally for the full and complete perfection of the beloved, "So that she may be holy and without blemish" (Eph 5:27). He makes it very clear that a Christian husband and wife are trying to achieve an other-centered love in which they can actually achieve the state of Eden: "They were naked and unashamed."

In their love passages spouses must constantly attempt to approximate the meaning designed by God (cf. Chapter 2 above).

Quite certainly, parents will not succeed in any kind of formation of their boys and girls to approximate the image of sexualness proportionate to each one's personhood if both have been involved in unrepented sexual sins and failures, and are full of guilts and remorse unresolved by penance, purpose of amendment, absolution and/or effective counseling. A man who is irresponsible, unfaithful to his wife, merely married to power and his place in the world, avaricious, and dishonest in his business, will hardly provide the model of responsible virility for his sons or a model of the kind of husbands his daughters should accept in prospect of marriage. He will be even less a model if his bedside reading is *Playboy, Hustler,* and *The Joy of Sex,* and his lecherous leers are a bone of contention for his wife; or worse, if his children have real reason to suspect that he is unfaithful to their mother; worst if his wife is but a mere service station, a receptacle for his lust, even if they are apparently ignorant of this. Chastity formation is impossible by someone who is himself unchaste. "What we are speaks so loudly, that they cannot hear what we say!" The warning bell or the bugle call to service will sound cracked from a damaged source.

On the other hand, a mother will hardly teach virginity to her girls and its desirability in a wife for her boys if she is carelessly seductive in her own home, openly flirts with other men, brings a boyfriend home, and her daughters can find her contraceptives in the medicine chest of the master bedroom, and observe her avidity for the "soaps" that celebrate all sorts of infidelity.

The ideal masculinity-femininity in spouses and parents here outlined is not to be considered merely an impossible dream. This ideal is the *norm* against which all activities should be *measured* with whatever failure to measure *up*. However, the ideal must be realistically and sympathetically presented to the children both in action and in word. A human male and female must be able to say to themselves, each one looking into the mirror of self, "You ain't much, baby, but you're the only me I've got!" and turn to the other to say, perhaps: "You may have failed, baby, but you're my only love." Indeed this last is what Jesus says to us in his mystical body! God is so "crazy" about us that He incredibly sent His Only Son to die on the cross for us, not *despite* our worthlessness, but *because* of it!

Francis Thompson tells us exactly in the poem "The Hound of Heaven" as Jesus speaks to him:

> Strange, piteous, futile thing!
> "Wherefore should any set thee love apart?
> Seeing none but I makes much of naught" (He said)
> "And human love needs human meriting:
> How hast thou merited —
> Of all man's clotted clay the dingiest clot?
>
> "Alack, thou knowest not
> How little worthy of any love thou art!
> Whom wilt thou find to love ignoble thee,
> Save me, save only me?

Realistic recognition of one's own failures to achieve or maintain chastity and modesty is of great value in one's sympathy with the struggles of one's own children. That father is to be praised who said, "Boy! Will I be glad when my children grow up old enough to know that I'm the one that needs correction!"

All this needs a tremendous sense of humor. The Good News, that is, the news that is too good to be true, is that God has given the grace to overcome temptation and sin and that He has already won for us through his death and resurrection the re-evaluation, "redemption," of all our sinful failures. Only a real Christian can truly laugh at himself. This awareness is the foundation of the truly Christian bawdy of Shakespeare and Chaucer (cf. the analysis in Thomas Howard's *An Antique Drum* [Philadelphia and New York: J.B. Lippincott Company, 1969] 120-124 and in *Sex Is Alive & Well*, H.V. Sattler, Ph.D. [Montrose, PA: Ridge Row Press, 10-20 S. Main Street, 1980] 111-112). The father is quite right who says to his son, "Never mind how I met your mother, just don't go around whistling, that's all!" It is quite correct for a close friend to tell the little girl that he knew her parents "before she was even a gleam in her father's eye." The humor evinced at weddings, which are suggestive of the pleasures of the marital bed is antidote for either too great a solemnity in approaching lovemaking or too obviously a leering lust. A child at such occasions should become aware, however vaguely, that there is some kind of special fun, celebration, and meaning that demands the warrant of marital commitment. The little girl is correctly approaching the meaning of Christian lovemaking when she asks, observing bride and groom kissing, "Is he sprinkling her with pollen now?" It is, however confusing to her, quite revealing that she know that there is a similarity but mysterious difference here between plants and humans, and that love and offspring go together. Paging through her parents' wedding album is her first "sex" or better, chastity education.

It should be apparent that no married couple or virginal and celibate man or woman has fully explained or explored the meaning of sexualness and sexuality in the spousal commitment of the body. Just as no one is ever a perfect knower, so no one is ever a perfect lover. Since the lovers are still growing and in self-appropriation of their body-love, they cannot give a perfect image to the observers or explain their progress to the neophyte in words. Parents, then, cannot wait until they have achieved sexual perfection before educating their children. They merely have to learn along with their children, because "our actions speak so loudly they cannot often hear what we say." This of course demands much apparently "wasted time" with children from the moment of conception. How a woman comes to terms with her pregnancy, and how her husband makes her feel lovable and loved during a time in which she finds her bodily ungainliness fearfully obscene to him, will form the child. I suspect how a woman resolves her multiple ambivalences towards being pregnant and the cause of her pregnancy and the cause of her problems in pregnancy (the child) will already have somewhat formed the child before its birth. How eagerly a mother puts the child to her breast and how approving her husband is of her devotion to this child, have a tremendous impact upon that child. If she is secure in his love for her, and is not suddenly expected to treat him as her oldest baby because of his jealously of the time she gives to his child, she will avoid passing on this psychic ambivalence to the baby.

Nor is there any such thing, especially for a mother, as "quality time." One cannot choose a premeditated moment in which to give love formation to a baby. We have found that a child must be fed on demand and so must his or her emotional needs be met at the moment they appear. Nor need the meeting of the child's emotional needs and questions be perfectly achieved. The *will* of the mother to form the child as best she can is more formative than the *skill* with which she does it. Often enough, technique or preplanned answers appear self-conscious and possibly phoney, whereas fumbling efforts repeatedly corrected in order to get it clear show total orientation and openness to the child.

It might be more difficult for a father to spend planned time with his child, but he must discover ways of doing so, and when he does deal with the child, it ought not to be from behind a newspaper or with one eye and ear on the TV set. Mothers learn to look their children directly in the eyes, and so should fathers!

Responsibility

Pope John Paul II suggests that it is a duty of the modern couple in marriage to become aware of what is called Natural Family Planning and which I prefer to call the freedom of Aware Parenting. If a woman becomes aware of her fertility cycle and her husband becomes aware of it with her, and she equivalently becomes aware of the meaning of his stronger sexual appetite, they can mutually take responsibility for each other: she to respond avidly to him, when they have decided to express their love sexually, and he to have the responsibility to seek their union only when they are aware of the relative probability of fertility and their willingness to open themselves, their beings, to this tremendous involvement! Natural family planning with mutual responsibility is the culmination of the celebration of love on the conjugal couch (cf. Sattler, *op. cit.*, "Celebrating Natural Family Planning," 114-117).

Only *logically* does the foregoing analysis come first. When our Lord responded to the question about divorce in the Old Testament, He said, "In the *beginning*, it [divorce] was not so." He did not mean that historically, in the order of time! He meant *in principle*, the way it is designed, it is not so. That persons do not achieve the fullness of two-in-one-flesh, or have never fully achieved it, does not destroy that basic reality, so one must pursue the value as an objective even though one never achieves it.

Therefore, even while parents are attempting to achieve the model of marital and spousal love, they must carry on the education of their children. The failure to realize this is why so many people fail to achieve any kind of sexual maturation in their children. They are afraid to humbly admit their own failures or humorously (and humor and humility come from the same word root), approach the struggles of their own egos, and those of the children. A good priest who preaches a homily is quite aware that no one in his audience is more in need of conversion than he is and that he is but preaching to himself and allowing his audience to listen in! His audience is quite aware that he does not preach from the eminence of finished perfection. They heard him explode at the altar boys! Once it is clear that the method of educating of parents to achieve the fullness of parenthood is the same as the method of educating the children and goes on at the same time, one can discuss a progressive method of educating the children, with the proviso that it be immediately understood that there is no time table in which a lesson is started and completed, no lesson plan, no examination that will prove that one has achieved the desired result, no lesson ever fully learned, no hope that the educative job will ever be completed, no step by step progress. It is not possible to say, "The stork brought you, now stop asking me questions." When the children stop posing verbal or implicit questions, they have stopped learning. Once a person has stopped learning and appropriating sexuality, he is equivalently dead and needs only to be buried.

Chapter IV

Step By Step In Sex Education

Once it is understood that there can be no chronological process, we can follow the growth of a child and suggest some areas for consideration, but leave them all open-ended to the ingenuity of the parents. A college degree in biology or a graduate degree in education or psychology is not required, and indeed scientific knowledge may get in the way of sexual formation! All that is needed is an attempt to continually respect the meaning of being-of-a-sex and to love the sex of oneself and the child in his or her development.

Shame

Shame is not the same as guilt. Guilt is the awful emotional experience of judging that one has deliberately and answerably done a despicable deed. It can be true guilt from a real sin or crime, or false guilt, a feeling without foundation in a truly evil deed! Dealing with true guilt is a matter of penitence. Dealing with false guilt is a matter of psychological therapy! But shame or embarrassment is hesitance, or fear to reveal the self or what is private or personal, and of invading such privacy in another. It is akin to modesty, reverence, or awe at what is sacred, inviolable or reserved to God. In our state of fallen nature, called original sin, shame is the emotional attitude that recognizes that one could easily use one's own body or the body of another as a *mere thing,* a *mere* object of pleasure. Shame or embarrassment belongs properly to every human being, man or woman, boy or girl, within marriage itself or before marriage. It is natural in the human person. It is shed only hesitantly, and perhaps with repeated reluctance, to the end of life. To a faithful, beloved and committed spouse, sacred scripture says: "You are an enclosed garden, my sister, my bride, an enclosed garden, a fountain sealed" (Song of Songs 4:12), and recognizes that either spouse may enter such an enclosure only with the warrant and reverential respect of the marriage covenant. It is this awareness which is celebrated by the wedding gown, the bridal veil, the marriage tent, the crushing of the mutually used glass beneath the heel. It is also celebrated by the humorously bawdy, at the wedding celebration, with the throwing of the bride's bouquet to the unmarried girls, and the groom's right to take the garter from the wife and toss it to the bachelors present.

It is this hesitance and embarrassment which makes it very difficult for a man to talk out with his son and his son with his father, as well as for the pubescent girl to talk out with her mother, and her mother with her, the new bodily experiences of growing up. The young man and young woman are experiencing their *unique* personhood as growing into sexual maturity. Despite the fact that this happens to every young man and young woman whose hormone levels have been elevated and triggered by the pituitary gland, the experience is absolutely unique and personal for each individual! It is too intimate — innermost — to be easily shared with another. Our present public discussion of all these matters insults and traumatizes the experience which, however universal among boys and girls, remains absolutely unique for each person. A young lady experiencing her first romantic day dreams and perhaps mooning over some gangly adolescent who doesn't even recognize her existence, neither easily sorts our her feelings nor communicates them to her mother, and not at all to her dad or brothers. A boyish adolescent struggling with sexual self-control in terms of spontaneous erections or nocturnal loss of seed, might even be tempted to take heroic measures to keep pajama and bed linen stains from the eyes of his mother. Though he can be reassured that she knows and understands, he does not want her to know! Ordinarily neither he nor she will refer to the mutually known fact, not out of fearful guilt or judgmental anxiety, but out of respect for the shame and embarrassment of personal awareness and intimacy.

Fathers and mothers are legitimately hesitant to bring up these things to their boys and girls individually, first of all, because they fear their own possible prurience in invading the child's privacy, which would be a kind of incest! Nor do they want to invite the child to enter into parental struggles for chastity before or within their own marriage, or bedroom! They legitimately do not wish their children to fantasize about their conjugal lovemaking *both* because it is an invasion of their own privacy *and* a possible stimulus to the turbulent passions of youth.

The mutual embarrassment is to be respected and listened to, yet, though the topic must be broached delicately and with the hesitation that flows from respect, it ought to be initiated. But privately, on a one-to-one basis. No later than at the beginning of 6th grade for girls, a mother ought to discuss potential motherhood with her daughter. This is first done by suggesting to the little girl to become aware that her bodily discharges will begin to vary; that in the not-to-distant future, some slippery mucus discharge will appear at her vaginal opening. This is not some infection or worrisome anomaly, it is the sign that she is about to ovulate for the first time. Ovulation, though it will perhaps happen irregularly, is the first signal of her budding maturity, her potential to be a unique beloved, her potential to marry and give God children. Along with this new change in her body will come her moodiness, her romantic daydreams, anxiety about being lovable, fear that no one will ever notice her, and that if *he* does, she will die of embarrassment. She will be interested in the development of an attractive and youthful figure, the development of her breasts, a kind of strange discomfort as she tries to appropriate what seems almost a new body — yet she will be disturbed if her feminine figure appears much earlier than that of her friends — or much later!

The pubescent girl should also be told about conception which, of course, she already knows, but now in terms of its orientation towards implantation in the wall of the uterus and the menstrual experience — the weeping of a disappointed womb when there is no conception — which happens irregularly at first, but with ever increasing regularity, approximating 28 days, as she matures. Some warning must indicate that though mucous discharge and menstruation may seem messy and menstruation frighteningly bloody, neither is any kind of hemorrhage or loss of essential bodily fluids. A mother should consider the wisdom of menstrual pads versus tampons and particularly the loss of the hymen or virginal membrane and its possible meaning to the young woman. It is really impossible to tell a mother what to say. Even the listing of the above suggestions somehow or other seems an invasion of privacy, but only because it is written. The experience is unique to the experiencer and the instruction is unique to the love between a mother and child. Nor need a father be brought into the discussion though it may be hinted that he is generally aware of what's going on.

The pubescent girl is not without passion but her passions tend to be *erotic* in the best sense (romance!), rather than libidinous. Libido is sexual drive — more apparent in male than female. She is *thrilled* by the possibility that another human being could be as central to herself as she is to herself and as important to her as she is important. This is why she wants to be attractive for she wishes to *be Beloved* (Adam's name for Eve!). Her basic temptation will be to draw attention from males by her dress and developing body. She must understand, gradually at least, that not every attractiveness is legitimate, that young men will not necessarily offer her the satisfaction of her dream to be beloved, but might merely wish to possess and use her as a body to satisfy their appetite of the moment (lust) without any wish to love or be in any way committed.

It is at the same time that the young lady might well be drawn to a romantic love affair with Jesus. She may well consider whether she is called to the religious life of virginity. Every religious novice experiences "falling in love."

It is at this point that it should be explained that there is a fundamental spousal meaning of the body. An individual comes from the hand of God with absolute uniqueness. God's love for him or her is a spousal love. That is, in creating this human person, God has said, "No one like you has ever come into the world for me, and no one but you will come into this unique relationship ever again. As a result, I expect you to love me above all things, with your whole mind and soul and strength, to the level of precluding every other love. I demand this from you, not for my sake but for yours, since you cannot be fully what I have created you to be unless you surrender yourself totally to my creative power. I wish you to return to me this total dedication, which I have given to you, either directly in a virginal state, surrendering yourself to me in love, both body and soul, or through such a person as I will call to accept your gift of total femininity in my name and in my place." This second in Christian matrimony. It is imperative that every child develop a fundamental self-worth built, not upon self-fulfillment, but upon a sense of being called to empty the self in a special love. Nobody can give the gift of love to God that each human being has been called into the world to give. At this point it is very important to present the child with adequate role models for identification. Surely a mother should hope to be a good point of identification for her daughter and a father should be a point of contrast between masculinity and femininity so that she can discover who she is and what kind of a man she ought to contrast herself with as her knight in shining armor, whether he be the heroic Christ, or the virile Christian husband. Unfortu-

nately, though we need saint models for young women, we tend to canon-
ize only spousal virgins and not spousal wives and mothers, i.e. those who
enter marriage and are experienced in true conjugal love and who have
achieved a fulfilling motherhood. Rock stars, soap operas and Judy
Bloom's novels are hardly effective for the sexual self-identification of
young women as Christian women, wives and mothers.

The Adolescent Boy

With whatever embarrassment and hesitation, a father ought to prepare his son about the early problems of adolescence, the first of which is
the spontaneous erection and nocturnal ejaculation along with the temptation to produce this intense pleasure deliberately by masturbatory actions.
He ought to challenge his son to recognize that all the power of burgeoning youth, muscular, intellectual, emotional, and sexual, tends to be chaotic unless it is disciplined. A boy's new-felt desire to be his own self-
starter, to be responsible for his own initiatives and carrying them out,
tends to make him rebellious and critical of all kinds of authority. This is
a good orientation in the sense that it leads to independence and responsible initiative! Eventually, the buck stops here! But like his ability to
throw a baseball very hard, control is more important than power. He
must be told that he will naturally be attracted to feminine bodies because
that is the orientation of a man towards a woman, which enables him to
become two-in-one flesh with her, so that his union will be *matrimony*,
the state of making a woman his wife and a mother. Incidentally, "marriage" is a masculine description, since it means "the way of a man with a
maiden" (Prov 30:19). Like the power to lift heavy weights, the freedom
to make up his own mind, the use of sexual power is a responsibility. He
must never use this power merely to satisfy himself, or to depersonalize a
woman whether in imagination, by looking through books which present
depersonalized female nudity, or by abusing any girl he is with as a mere
means to his own satisfaction, no matter how willing she might be to be
so used! He is responsible for the control and positive use of freedom and
power. He must answer for her welfare if he wants to be virile. He is
responsible for the control and direction of his sexual power towards the
complete total gift of self to his wife and the acceptance of her total gift to
him. It is his potential fatherhood which will make him to be truly a man.
This same answerableness will be expected of him later in his possible

marriage, when long abstinence might be expected of him because of his wife's illness, the complications of pregnancy, or even because they truly agree to practice Aware Parenting (or Natural Family Planning).

Just as all control of power demands long practice and self-discipline, so does the control of sexual appetite. A father should sympathize with his adolescent's struggles and explain to his youngster, as well as to himself, that long years of sexual self-discipline are necessary beforehand, in order to test his ability for total dedication to another person, whom he will make central to his own being — in love.

Every boy knows that there is a test of virility to be passed during adolescence, whether it is the test of weight lifting, football, baseball, or emotional or moral heroism. Just as for the girl, now is the time to talk to the young man about his sense of vocation. God calls him into the world as a result of a love for the kind of virile service he wishes the new person to contribute directly to God or to a wife and children in the founding, leadership, protection, support, and direction of his family. To be called to follow Jesus as his leader demands the possibility of celibacy. Celibacy does not merely mean the absence of sexual release. It means the integration of one's person in all its power in pursuit of clear goals. Matt Dillon and the stars of all the old "horse operas" model celibacy in the pursuit and defense of frontier justice. Jesus is the example par excellence of complete self-control of almighty power in the service and leadership of love. He clearly indicates that He could easily have led a legion of angels to defend Himself against Romans and Jewish Sanhedrin, but He chose not to do so. He teaches with authority, but not defensively, as do the scribes and pharisees with all their rationalizations and arguments. He drives the money changers from the temple of His Father. They are frightened of His strength. He founds the church upon a weak and vacillating Peter, whom He nevertheless calls and makes to be the *rock* of authoritative teaching, He sends an infant Church into a hostile world to tell that world "the way it is" and the way it's got to be, despite the martyrdom which faced all of them, and the disbelief that will always dog His faithful ones. He established a Church in which the weak were always to be protected and served by the strong. This sense of being called to virile fulfillment is exerted whether in the priestly or religious life, as a single person in the world because no suitable partner to whom one feels called to respond crosses his paths, or as the leader and head of a new Christian family.

A father must teach his son that he has a great desire of endless sexual curiosity as a result of original sin and that this desire to see and touch and experience will never die. But, that Our Lord tells him what he must do. "If your eye causes you to stumble, tear it out" (Mk 9:47)! Again, every human male is desirous of touching and exploring a female body. This touch is designed to enable him to express love for his wife and to discover her fullness as he would his own body, but this exploration is more for her fulfillment as wife and mother and not just for his own satisfaction. Though touch may say "mine" this possessiveness implies total responsibility for the other, not selfish use. So "If your hand causes you to stumble, cut it off" (Mk 9:43)! Of course, Jesus does not expect a person to maim himself. What He is saying is: "If looking leads you to lust, don't look! If touching leads you to use another for your own sexual satisfaction, don't touch!"

If he cannot *say* what lovemaking *says* — absolute, total self-gift of one man to one woman for a lifetime with the willingness to accept the risk of a child — he may not initiate what he is not permitted to complete. As role models we should propose to adolescents not only the great martyrs and great missionaries who were freed from family life in order to conquer new worlds at a distance, but also those married saints or even those struggling men of his acquaintance who exemplify true virility.

Every young men should see and ponder the "Man For All Seasons," and later, "Man of LaMancha." A son should be challenged to be able to express affection and eventually give a girl a hug and a kiss in warm tenderness, and still be responsible for delivering her to her home after a date or an outing, intact and not feeling mauled, manipulated, seduced or blackmailed into giving herself or permitting herself to be used for his own satisfaction. The boy should be further reminded that a girl's desire for love and affection, for hugging, cuddling and to be held, is in no way an invitation for the sexual touching which is the ordinary preliminary for that two-in-one-ness which belongs only to the absolute and irrevocable commitment of husband to wife and wife to husband. Then, he will not be surprised later in marriage to find that a wife who wants to be held does not necessarily desire intercourse.

Finally the young boy should be reminded that the struggle is long and never fully achieved even in marriage. There are sinful failures. It takes prayer and frequent approach to the Sacrament of Reconciliation, meditation upon the weakness of human nature and the glory of matrimony and celibacy poured out in love-service to God, and approach to the Body of Christ in the Eucharist, which will recognize that sinful failures are not failures of the self alone but a failure which also sullies the Body of Christ, since we are members of His Body (cf. St. Paul especially in 1 Cor 6 and 12; Eph 4, and Jesus Himself, when He tells us that what we have done to others we have done to Him, in Mt 25: 40 and ff.).

Since the use of virility is a matter of divine vocation of being called by God, either to celibacy or to marriage, the young man should early be taught by his father to pray for clear vision of the direction to which he is being called, and equally to pray that should he be called to marriage that he will find a young woman who will share his vision of love service and help him to achieve his as he will help her to achieve hers. Please God, he should be able to sing, "I want a girl, just like the girl that married dear old dad" — not with mawkish sentimentality, but with the deepest love and respect.

A boy should not generally be pushed into becoming interested in girls. For him, the meeting is one of intense and serious responsibility, and he should not be encouraged to enter into it, until he is ready to assume the responsibilities it entails.

Someone has suggested that the temptation to self-abuse or masturbation, which afflicts every average growing boy is so terribly strong precisely to teach the real value of sex! If sexual union is the total unconditional gift of self to one who responds equally, it demands a gift without focus on the giver but upon the receiver. One only learns gift-love when he sacrifices his own desires. A boy gives his very first gift to his mother, when he uses his carefully hoarded money, saved for a desired toy, to purchase it. Without doing without, he cannot really possess what he wishes to give. Without the struggle for self-control one cannot be self-possessed enough to give the self to one's spouse.

Boy Meets Girl — Girl Meets Boy

By the time the girl has finished the sixth grade, she is generally very, very interested in boys, but the boys do not even know that she is alive until they are some two years older. It is a good thing that boys and girls are critical of each other within their own homes. A girl with an older brother is very rapidly corrected if her dress is seductive, or her actions "sexy." The same thing that attracts him to get out of line with someone else is the very thing that he wishes to protect his sister against! On the other hand, an older sister will be very critical of the girls her younger brother brings home, if only to prevent him from making a fool of himself. Again, older brothers will be protective of their sisters against the Don Juans they might be aware of or suspect among those who meet their sister.

As girl meets boy and boy meets girl, the girl should become aware of her tremendous *eductive* power over the boy. The word *eductive* will probably not be found in the dictionary. It means the ability to draw *out* a potential. A girl's ability to draw out the potential of a boy is either *super*ductive, ability to draw him to supreme achievement, or *se*ductive, ability to draw him *down* to utter destruction! It is a tradition for a young woman to boast of her ability to twist a man around her little finger. Sometimes mothers are actually jealous of their little girl's ability to do that with dad, just what they themselves are most effective at in winning the love of their husbands! A boy's power is more muscular strength, force, and external initiative and accomplishment. Both sorts of power must be put to the service of others.

In this connection, a young lady must learn that her natural desire to attract may destroy the self-control of a boy and actually lead him to do what she will most resent when he does it. Modesty of dress need not conceal feminine charms, but should not display them for every passerby's lust. A girl wishes all sorts of signs of affection and is willing to permit ever advancing liberties if they seem affectionate. On his side, a boy will perceive her willingness to follow his lead as inviting him to the kind of familiarity which belongs only in marriage. Again, a boy can easily be tempted to offer a companion all signs of affection, kissing, cuddling, and hugging, in order to achieve his goal of sexual conquest. This is a cynical manipulation of her for his own lust. Note that the word "familiarity" means "being at home with." Bodily familiarity with another demands the privacy of a conjugal home.

The boy must learn that not every response is an invitation to violate her personhood by sexual intimacy, and that she must understand that not every apparent romantic sign of affection from him need be what it appears to be. Both sides are frequently guilty of bartering the one for the other: he, apparent affection for sexual release; she, apparent sexual avidity for romantic affection. This is particularly necessary information for both adolescent boys and girls: that at the moment of affection's most intense moments, the male tends to wish direct skin contact (called petting). The question both sides must ask, is "May I wish to express the kind of love which the action I am drawn to do really says?" If the signs of affection are truly such with only incidental and unintentional sexual stirrings as side effects, the action may possibly be justified. If the action says "Mine", "Yours", or is the stirring preliminary to the meaning of sexual intercourse, the activity is always sinful and seductive of them to act out the total mutual sexual gift which is the spousal gift of matrimony, when they are in no condition to carry out and measure up to the responsibilities of its meanings.

Finally it is imperative for father to explain to his son and mother to her daughter the meaning of sexual intercourse itself. (Cf. above pp. 16 ff.)

Conclusion

In all the above, it should be apparent that there is little or no need for parents to teach the biology of cells, the physiology of erection, penetration and ejaculation, the mechanics of tumescence and detumescence, the physiological process of implantation, pregnancy, breast feeding, and nurturing. Nor is there generally any need to initiate discussion of sexual life-styles, sexual promiscuity, sexual perversions, homosexuality, the sexual wilderness in which we live, pornography, incest, rape, contraception, or even venereal diseases. The whole concern of proper sex education of parents for children, must be towards a reverence for the earthy reality of the human body as masculine or feminine and the meaningfulness of that body as a sign of the spousal gift of the human person from God and back to Him whether directly or through the vocational presence of a spouse. When the other things come up, as they inevitably will, the response will already be prepared for. The reason parents and the Church are losing the battle for Christian sexual morality is that they are always defensive against a question such as: "Why can't I do what I am attracted to? What's wrong with it?" Only if there is a right or correct way to live can the incorrect, erroneous or evil way be clarified. We are losing the battle against drug abuse and addiction because we have no ideal of sobriety, alertness. We will never achieve "no!" to drugs if we allow a feeling of euphoria be our goal (instant "feel good") instead of the happiness of achievement, or better, of lending our efforts to indefinitely pursuable goals such as life, truth, human service, artistic and practical creativity, friendship, peace, justice, marital love, procreativity, mothering and fathering.

This does not mean that educated parents might not impart some of the biological, physiological, medical, and genetic information which might be of help to their children, but these kinds of knowledge are not essential to adequate formation of a child to face life, or else one would have to conclude that sex education has never ever adequately been performed, that there have never been happy men, women, marriages or family life since it takes a minimum of a bachelor's degree in sexology to have sufficient information!

Studies which use questionnaires about the adequacy of sex education always tout the apparent ignorance of respondents. No one has ever been found who admitted he had an adequate knowledge about the mysteries of sexualness and sexuality! But how has the knowledge of graafian follicles or the epididymis ever affected the ordinary day to day living of two people who enter into a loving marriage? How has statistical knowledge of the frequency of illicit orgasm helped devoted couples?

The above material itself, in it's attempt to abstract a sexual education from the general education of children by parents, fails by spending all its time and space on sexual reality which is but one, however all-penetrating, fiber in masculine or feminine personhood. If any reader attempted to follow the above suggestions consciously, or from a formal memorization, he or she would fail miserably and deservedly, in the very kind of sex education which this book attempts to inculcate! Chastity and modesty as well as celibate and married nuptial love cannot be *taught* from formal disciplines. They must be *caught* from word, tonality, attitude, emotional expression, self-respect, respect for the bodies of others, love of friends, love of others, marital expressions of affection, joy in the birth of a new child, and even from the wise shame, embarrassment and modesty, or even guilts, that are experienced in one's own fumbling attempts to achieve ever more meaningful sexual identity, activity, control, commitment, dedication.

Chapter V

Parents And The Direct Sex Education Of The Children

The child has already begun to be directly formed by the conjugal love of the parents from the moment of their falling in love, because their love is essentially a mutual surrender to each other and to whatever comes. Mutual unconditional surrender is the meaning of marriage, "for better or for worse." Procreating, then, is the action in which there is unconditional surrender to whatever might arrive by way of a conception, of whatever "quality of life," or factual life history a child might achieve. Education is merely procreation extended. It is surrender to whatever might be discovered of potential to be drawn forth from the child. How the parents accept their pregnancy (and the pregnancy is mutual) is apparent to the child. A woman who is uneasy with her pregnancy, rejective, angry, discontented, without resolving the negative in favor of the positive attitudes, without resolving her quite natural human ambivalence, will have an effect on the child. How her husband treats her during this time will have similar impact. I cannot prove that this begins while the child is in the uterus, but I know that the child is a human person from conception. I know that some morning sickness is due to unconscious rejection of pregnancy by a mother and since I know that the child's nervous system gets a very early start, I would not be surprised if the child is already a little bit aware at least of his acceptance in the womb. It has been reported by several very introspective psychoanalysts, undergoing their own analysis, that they have been able to recall incidents *in utero.* I myself have a recurrent nightmare which could well be interpreted as a memory of the rending of the amniotic sac (the so-called "bag of waters") and the trauma of birth.

Granting that the ideal situation is seldom perfectly achieved, the deliberate sex education of the child begins at the moment of birth. If the mother goes through a labor which she sees clearly as exhausting but worthwhile hard work (labor), if her husband can honestly be present to second her efforts and coach them, if the child can be put immediately to breast upon delivery, its fundamental self-acceptance and its so called "imprinting" or "bonding" (which is true even for animals) is begun. We do not know but suspect that there is much more deeply psychological meaning for human beings than the sensitive meaning for animals. The separation from the mother who is unconscious due to anesthesia, and who will meet the child only a day or so later must certainly be traumatic for the child and thoroughly overcompensated for, if it is not to have its impact upon the child. All the hugging and kissing and fondling as well as the skin contact with the baby, especially in the process of nursing at the breast, is an early contributor to self-acceptance — of the body and of sex!

Before Questioning

Before an infant can ask his or her first questions, there are many avenues of adequate sex education. If the mother and father dress the child in characteristic masculine or feminine fashion and praise the child for being attractively manly or womanly, long before the child understands the words that are uttered, he grasps something of the "music." The mother who in despair scotch-taped a ribbon to her baldpated little girl was giving very effective sex education.

When dealing with the bodily needs of the child, parents communicate how they feel about masculinity and femininity. The bodies of little boys are made differently than the bodies of little girls. Older children may observe these differences as the child is bathed and changed, or as they carry out this care themselves, with the simple explanation that this is the way it is. Boys and girls differ in these anatomical ways as a fact to be noted and accepted.

Early on the child will begin to explore his body and find out how far he goes and what is "I" and what is "not I." (At first he objectifies himself as "me!") This exploration is innocent in itself, but needs early direction. A mother finds it in no way difficult to correct a child for putting things in his nose, ears, or mouth that ought not to be there. She should have no more concern, but no less, when the child wishes to put something in her vagina. A parent early observes the little boy in erection. It has been reported that by ultrasound photography, the erection can be observed even in utero. How strange that the sexologists use this fact to suggest the child's "birthright" to sexual experience, while refusing to accept the film called the "Silent Scream" as evidence of the evil of abortion!

Far from being disturbed at this early stirring, parents must realize that the equipment for sexual stimulus is present, that resultant excitation can happen by accident, but should not be deliberately triggered by the parents, baby sitter, or external stimulus, lest the child become already accustomed to the kind of pleasure seeking that will eventually become uncontrollable. Surely a little boy should not be propped up in front of a TV screen presenting scantily clad majorettes. His reaction will be stronger than any adult male's who should have learned a bit of inhibition! The little girls can be kept very attractive and feminine without being praised for being sexy. Sexy means stimulative of sexual arousal and desire for lustful experience.

It is interesting that our modern sexologists are becoming quite schizoid. They insist that sexual release is always good even in the womb, but they are quite concerned (illogically) about child abuse and incest. Why! If orgasm is a good in itself what can be wrong about teaching and encouraging children to achieve it? Only if sexual release is meaningful in certain ways, and perverse in others, can there be a reason to call sexual inculcation "abuse." Nutritious food is to be made tasty. It is wrong to encourage the pursuit of every "taste treat."

Where Did I Come From?

The earliest questions of the child are focused upon suspicion that he could fall out of being (which is the basis of all fright or fear, for example, of the dark) and that there is a source of his being outside himself (God). When he asks "Where did I come from?", it is not a question about his biological origin. An early "organ recital" is not the answer! This is the time to tell him that he came from God, that God made him, but it is also the time to delight the child with every imaginative and delightful fantasy which focuses on the miracle of unique, irrevocable and forever personhood. One mother (college grad married to an MD!) was urged by her obstetrical nurse to give her 2 1/2 year old little girl biological details. The mother refused because, said she, "Sarah has a better story than I can tell her." Her little girl had concocted a fantastic fairy tale of a playmate on the other side of the stars ready to come down to play with her. She was quite aware of her mother's extended abdomen and the presence of her new brother or sister there, but simply refused to consider it.

When the time seems right, and only a mother can know the time, it is time to bring out the wedding pictures and show that, along with God's love, this is where the child came from, from the love of husband and wife!

The reason that this is so important is that the child needs a tremendous sense of security. And security is discovered only by the certainty of being loved, the certainty that the child is sourced in love, and the further certainty that that source will never dry up! God will always be God, Mother and Father will never stop loving each other. And if that love should fail, or be imperfect as inevitably it must, parents must admit to their children that they don't always like them, and they know that the children do not always like the parents, but that God will always love the child. "Can a woman forget her nursing child, or show no compassion for the child of her womb? Even these may forget, yet I will never forget you. See, I have inscribed your name on the palms of my hands" (Isaiah 49:15).

A problem immediately arises if the child has been adopted. Has this person been rejected by his natural parents? Or perhaps a mother or father has been divorced or separated? Has the unpresent, absent parent been unfaithful to the child? Has the child done anything to cause the lack of love which he knows to be at the basis of all his security as a person? How to answer these questions in both an honest way so that the child will learn that love is necessary but that nobody achieves either the giving or receiving of it perfectly is important.

The child must be taught very early that not having been loved should not be responded to by not loving in return, or by hatred. Hatred never destroys the person who seems evil, it only destroys the hater! It is important for the child to know what St. John teaches us, that God loved us *first*, that we were loved into being, and that though we ought also to be loved first by parents in order to come into and continue in being, every human being must learn to love first, even before he demands love. This is why Jesus tries to teach us to love our enemies and to do good to those who hate us (Lk 6:27). Though it is true that a child ought never to experience feeling unloved or a feeling of being rejected or hated, he cannot achieve this because each person is unique with needs that are not clearly known either to a lover, or to himself. He will also be, and suspect that he is to some extent, inadequately loved. The "me" generation has not yet discovered that fulfillment lies in emptying the self and not in being filled. A paradox! "Unless the grain of wheat falls into the ground, it dies and remains alone, but if it dies it brings forth fruit a hundredfold. He who *keeps* his life in this world, loses it, and he who *loses* his life in this world, keeps it, even to life everlasting (Mt 16:25). It is indeed better to give than to receive" (Acts 20:35).

It is indeed apparently cruel that a child should have to be taught this very early in life, because of some human lapse by someone who ought to have accepted and loved him, but it must be learned. An adopted child or even an abandoned child must learn to be grateful at least for existence, to understand the weakness of human failure, to beware of his own infidelities to love in the present or in the future. Ultimately he must throw himself upon God. No finite human creature can ever be absolutely trusted, because he cannot know all my innermost emptinesses, and if he knew them he would be helpless to fill every one of them. Everyone must sing: "Sometimes I feel like a motherless child" or "You always hurt the one you love," or cry "With lovers like I have who needs enemies?"

Physical Descriptions

Fairy tales are wonderful analyses of the mysteries of life, of good and evil. If only they were truly *tales*. A stork story about the burgeoning of new life after a hard deadly winter in Holland, where the storks nested in the chimneys in order to keep their eggs warm enough for the chicks to hatch, was and perhaps is still, a lovely way to explain the squalling of the new infant in the home below. We use newborn bunnies and chicks breaking through their shells to explain the resurrection of Jesus Christ. A farm child knows quite well that he was not found in the cabbage patch under a large cabbage leaf and he pretty well understood that though the doctor came to his house (or the midwife), he did not carry the new baby in a little black bag. But these were not lies, they were "put offs," and there are indeed times in which a child can reasonably be put off so long as he does not perceive that the question is never to be asked at all, but only at a more opportune time.

Bodily descriptions can be invasive of privacy and the natural modesty of the child. They can also be frightening, if their vividness is disconcerting or traumatic. Finally they can be very stimulative, inhabit dreams or nightmares, be utilized in fearsome fantasies, and, in the sexual area, be the source of such sexual arousal as the child or adult may not be able to cope with. For this reason, metaphors, tales, or more romantic images may be a necessary substitute for either matter-of-factness or vividly portrayed and often gory details. Modesty or moderation is the designation for thoughtful awareness of the body and its functions as well as what happens to it.

Bodily modesty should be taught to both sexes rather early. A child discovers a concept of self and the need to protect it very early. He wants his own clothes, his own toys, his own dishes, perhaps his own blanket. He likes to play hide and seek (a game of privacy and self-revelation!). All these are building a sense of self, which is at base a sense of privacy. Though his mother will despair that he or she will ever learn to close the bathroom door, there will come a time when a childish cry "Mommy, Jimmy wants to come in here" will indicate the longed for moment of the sense of privacy. Since genitality is at the *center* of personhood, as expressed in the body, the refusal to have one's genitals viewed or fondled should be quietly taught very early. After years of attack upon bodily modesty we are now becoming aware of the danger of child abuse once again! Some are even teaching a (horrors!) puritanical concept of "good touch" and "bad touch." With such education, how will they accept of conjugal touch and exploration in marriage? Touching is not good or bad in itself. It is "touch out of place" which is dangerous. In the "good touch" "bad touch" approach, a child can get all sorts of scrupulous conscience and fears. One touches oneself in bathing and micturition, genitally, without concern. Touch must be explained as necessary in parental, nursing, and medical care.

As soon as the child is able to bathe himself or herself adequately, the mother should gradually retire from the activity except for necessary inspection for cleanliness. This can easily be taught by praise for progressive growing up that goes along with the desire to be in control of oneself (urination and potty training), to dress oneself and button up. Of course, modesty within the home is not the same as modesty towards those without. It would be an unusual little boy who had never caught a glimpse of his sister scurrying from bathroom to bedroom because she had forgotten a fundamental article of clothing. Again, the example of parents is paramount. Wives and husbands should not read each other's personal mail. One's "things" should not be arbitrarily appropriated. It is a well designed house for a family of husband, wife and a number of children, whose rooms have doors which are regularly closed! It might be a good idea in preadolescence for a room full of brothers to post an "Off Limits" sign to parents on their bedroom door.

Modesty And Medicine — Bodily Facts

Biology and physiology are sciences abstracted from real living animals. Biology is the study of the start, nourishment and division of cells. The biologist implicitly accepts that there is no real distinction, no real difference, between an amoeba, through the kingdom of living realities, and the human being, except a difference in degree and complexity. For him the higher level of animality merely points to the greater complexity of the genetic material in the RNA. His interest in sex is basically an interest in meiosis and recombinant DNA. (What? you don't know or have you forgotten what meiosis is? Forget it!)

Physiology is the study of the functioning of human anatomy. Since we conceive of most functions as instrumental, when we use instruments, their instrumentality depends upon our own imaginative goals and the proportionate effectiveness of these activities to such goals. But bodily activity in the area of sex education is not in the area of biology and function but is more in the area of *semantics* and *symbolism* and involves meaning and morality! One discovers very little about drunkenness and intoxication from the physiology or the biology of nerve cells ingesting alcohol. One discovers very little about human copulation from the biology of sperm and egg and the physiology of animal coitus!

The human being is different from all other living realities, not only in degree but in kind, and in kind radically — from the root up. Affection between a mother and a child, manifested by a mutual nibbling is not merely animal affection at base, with an over-coating of free love choice which is human. Affectivity which is sensible in a bodily way for human beings is utterly transformed by the free choice of will which we call love. It is quite natural for children to anthropomorphize their pets, to personalize them by giving them names and by speaking of them as though the relationship from male to bitch, and of bitch to puppies, is identically the relationship between human father and mother and both of them with a child. But though we can *metaphorically* praise the bitch's devotion to her litter of pups as "being a good mother," the dog's function is entirely instinctual whereas a mother's function with her children is a responsible choice to which she measures up or fails. The bodily involvement in begetting and bearing and raising children is in no way identical with the body involvement of conceiving, whelping, feeding and weaning of puppies. This is the reason that many a farm teenager, active in 4-H, might be quite deliberately but unconsciously ignorant of human generation, despite the fact that he or she has presided over the breeding and delivery of prize farm animals. Even the vulgar obscenity which draws the self-conscious joking about human sex reveals that it is utterly distinct, and very special. If human procreating activity were identical with animal coitus, there would be nothing surprising about it and there would be no vulgar, obscene, offensive or lustful terms nor shame, modesty or guilty self-consciousness! Nor would there be any desire for privacy in such activity, for surrounding it with ritual, protocol, warrants, liturgies and religious protection.

This does not indicate that biology, anatomy and physiology should not be taught on every school level in the scientific fashion which is appropriate to the abstract discussion on the level of student understanding. How the heart works, or digestion takes place, and reproduction is achieved can be treated on every level in equivalent fashion, but one does not talk about the physiology of the heart palpitation upon falling in love, nor does he bring the description of defecation to explain the banquet table, or the physiology of sex to explain the yearning of a man and a woman to become two-in-one flesh (two-in-one person) or to open himself to the cooperation with God in the begetting of a son or daughter. The discussion of parents with their children about the origin of the new human person is therefore not a matter of biology, anatomy or physiology, but a matter of bodily significance. A wink, a smile, a lie, a slap, a kiss, a hug, are not explained by the physiological musculature involved. Neither are the carrying of a baby, the becoming of two-in-one-flesh, the conception of a new human being, the birthing of a child or its nursing. If a young woman knows the meaning of breast feeding, by her experience as baby and by her observation of the loving concern of her mother with a new child, she will know that her breasts are primarily for nurturing and only secondarily to attract the love which will make of her virginity a mothering! If parental formation is for girls to be women, for boys to be men, and for their positive attitude toward mutual surrender in matrimony, then bodily facts are meaningful or significative, not scientific!

They physical attraction of breast and bottom is towards mothering, and only instrumentally towards sexual arousal.

Pregnancy

When the child first asks "where did I come from?" and is not satisfied with "God made you," or "The love of daddy and mommy brought you here," it is time to speak of pregnancy, which is a communication experience rather than a biological one. After all, we are rapidly discovering how we can take care of even human biological life *in vitro*, in test tubes, in incubators and germ free plastic bubbles, but somehow we perceive that this is not the way it ought to be from the human and personal point of view. Else why do we laugh at the cartoon, which shows a huge test tube in the corner of a laboratory to which one scientist refers in telling another inquirer, "Oh that's for the woman who wants the basketball player." Or when a veterinarian MD suggests that a husband become "psychologically involved" (jargon term for loving involvement of persons) in the artificial insemination by "pushing the plunger!" No one thinks it is funny to ask the vet to push the plunger for an angus cow! And yet we would see some poetic justice should the angus bull escape the semen milker and gore the vet's new Cadillac, because we see the incongruity that would be involved in substituting a syringe for *human* love union. To the question of pregnancy, the first answer on a bodily level: the baby starts within the mother's body, where there is a place like a little room or nest where it will be safe until it grows big enough to grow outside her body. As early as possible the child should know that this place is called a *womb*, if only because it provides an explanation for that mysterious prayer: "Blessed is the fruit of thy womb, Jesus." But it is pedantic to insist that the little child say that the baby is in the mother's *abdomen*. Tummy is the child's word! And though it is not physiologically correct, it is not surprising that the child says *stomach* too. Scientific exactness is irrelevant! The meaningfulness of being "with child" is what is important. Notice the games that mothers play with their babies. "I could hug you to death. . . I could eat you up. . . How much do you love mommy?. . . So big. . . Squeeze tight." A mother wants her baby to be inside her because the experience of another person as central to herself as she is to herself is called L-O-V-E. This is the *identical* experience she has had with her husband in starting the child. Surely a young child should be allowed to feel the movements of his little brother or sister within mother's womb. Or maybe to help her to listen to its heartbeat. Perhaps picture books of pregnancy might well be introduced, but they should be meaningful in a romantic sort of way. Neither as abstract as diagrammatic biology nor as concrete as to be simply messy.

All the misunderstandings of the child which burst forth in such surprising questions should just be a source of family hilarity rather than of anxiety or of fright. If a child wonders whether the baby will explode with a loud pop, or whether mother started him by swallowing something, there is no reason to be perturbed about his error. On the other hand, a parent should not respond to a child's question if the answer seems to be embarrassing to either herself or the child. Embarrassment or shame is a kind of modesty that does not flow from guilt, but from respect for one's own person or the personhood of the child. After one has matured the child enough to close the bathroom door, one is embarrassed to enter while the child takes care of bodily needs, and is equally embarrassed to be burst in upon by the child. So also if the question seems to invade the privacy of the mother or father, or the answer somehow seems to them to invade the privacy of the child, it ought not to be answered. To force an answer because some expert has insisted that this is the way it should be done at a certain time is to do it with discomfort, and it will make the recipient uncomfortable too. And what is uncomfortably said does not ring true, but sounds phoney, false.

How Does The Baby Get Out?

A mother or father can explain to a child that there is a special opening between the mother's legs which enlarges sufficiently to enable the baby to get out. As one mother explained to her little girl: "There are three openings, one for pee, one for pooh, and one for the baby." This subtly leaves open an awareness of how the baby started too. Printed here this may well make the reader uncomfortable, as any private intimate utterance would when posted on the bulletin board! I publish it here just to help the reader to accept both the intimacy and the healthy meaning of shame!

Birthing is the experience called labor — worthwhile hard work. This is an occasion to describe and commiserate with Our Lord who said in anticipation of the miracle of His death and triumphant resurrection, that a woman when she is in labor is sad because her hour is at hand. But when the child is born she is glad that a man is born into the world (Jn 16:21). How accurate an analysis! It is unrealistic to romanticize the difficulty of birthing, and equally unrealistic to traumatize the child by frightening him. And yet it can be explained about how frightened he sometimes feels in the dark, and alone or seemingly alone when he is sick or sad. How good to feel that mommy and daddy are close as he travels alone in the dark which is what each of us had to do again and again. Though it is not true that mothers go down to death's door to give birth to their children, in the sense of risking their lives, they do go down to the fundamental nitty-gritty of being alive, and of where the most earthy of existence is. Some mothers want their husbands to be with them at the moment of the birth of their child, to encourage and share. Other mothers want their husbands to be as far away as possible because when they come to this elemental kind of living, they do not want him to observe their weaknesses, coming apart at the seams or even their tears (or expletives!).

I know of a couple who show slides, carefully selected, of the actual birth of their children to the children themselves and to their brothers and sisters. The impact upon these children is electric. It leads them to joy, pity, commiseration, tears and happiness but one would be very hesitant to show the entire process in motion pictures as obviously too traumatic for the immature child. It is interesting that this set of parents discusses and decides on each occasion whether to show the slides and which slides to show and which to omit! It has been a different decision each time. Only the parents themselves can make this sort of judgment. This should not be a school room vis-ed program.

Nursing

Breast nursing can be explained simply to the other children by observation and comment as needed, but need not be ostentatious. Perhaps not so strangely, I have never observed anyone lusting at breast nudity over a woman nursing her child, even by a man given to breast fetishism. The questions about nourishment, about the size of the breast and its function, about why little boys do not have breasts, and little girls do not yet have them, are simply too numerous to answer here. Warmth towards the begetting process and feeding by mother and father will easily discover answers that will be embarrassing to no one. Humor and laughter *with* (not *at*) childish mistakes and misapprehensions will dispel any possible tensions.

Delicacy

Again and again one hears that the process of sex education is in areas of very delicate concern. One should wonder why we consider certain questions delicate! We do not consider questions about other bodily processes delicate, though we might consider them vulgar. No one suggests that education in literature or grammar or mathematics is delicate. Nor on the social virtues of citizenship or public spirit. Why do we suggest that areas of love and procreation are delicate matters? There are two reasons for this.

The first is that the sharing of bodies, the becoming of two-in-one-flesh and the awesome responsibility of risking a new human person into the world are too intimate, too private, to be easily invaded or easily discussed. The very matter of modesty in clothing and indeed the existence of clothing at all, sets the human person, whether man or woman, completely apart from the animal kingdom. One does not wear another's underwear, open and read his letters, demand a recounting of his fantasies, burst in upon him in the bathroom. This kind of hesitance is greatly missed when custom destroys it. The nudity of the barracks or of gang showers is more or less depersonalizing and even in the separate sex dressing rooms, individuals of the same sex tend to avert their eyes from their neighbor's bodies. It is the rare man or woman who is not embarrassed to some extent even by a necessary physical examination by a trusted and loved physician. Sometimes we even prefer a stranger so that we will not have to meet him or her in any personal fashion outside of the examining room.

Perhaps, we ought also to go back to the darkness and screen of the confessional because it is always as difficult to get morally "undressed" before someone as it is physically. This is the reason that the conjugal couch is the only fitting place for the confession of faults and infidelities.

The second reason why sexual questions are embarrassing is because every individual knows his or her sensitivity to sexual arousal, fears arousing it in anyone else, and particularly in a respected, loved, or dependent person. A lecherous man who obviously undresses with his eyes a seductively clad passerby might turn to his daughter and say, "If you ever wear anything like that, I'll beat your ears in." His words will fall on deaf ears. The same man who tells locker room tales, will hesitate to share them with anybody he loves and never gets to talk to his son in any sympathetic manner about how to deal with his temptations! Because his speech can only be hypocritical or phoney. The incest taboo is often, and correctly, inhibitory of discussion on sexual matters between parents and a child.

If, then, we are convinced of the delicacy of certain sexual discussions, we ought never to attempt to overcome our hesitance to the point of ignoring it. After Adam and Eve decided to make up their own rules of right and wrong, they discovered for the first time that they had lost the self-control necessary to follow the truly fulfilling sexuality of man and woman. They noticed that they were naked and sewed for themselves loincloths of fig leaves (Gn 3:7).

Sexual Union

The questions which have bodily answers of "Where did I come from" and "How did the baby get out" are not "delicate" in themselves. They are only delicate in the orientation towards the next two questions: "How did the baby get there in the first place?" and "What is this new, strange, disturbing experience in my body?" In answer to the question of "How did the baby get into the mother's body in the first place?", it is necessary to make the child aware, that though God made Adam and Eve without any help from anybody else, Adam from the dust of the earth, and Eve from Adam's innermost "heart of his heart", He wanted them to become two-in-one flesh so that they might cooperate with Him in begetting children. God did something wonderful for Adam and Eve, He let them help Him make their children, and ever since then, God has asked men and women to help Him to bring children into the world. He was very good in His plan for this and it was a great idea, for He didn't need the help of people. He could have made each individual child the way He made Adam and Eve without anybody's help. Indeed He is still specially involved in the coming to be of every person. And that is why helping God to have a new child to adore Him, to become a part of the real body of Christ and to belong not only to parents but to the Church, God reserves the way in which a body gets started in its mother's body to a special state called matrimony. This is a big word which means the sacred or holy way of making a mother. It takes three to start a baby, God, the mother and the father. If any one of them were to be missing, there would be no baby. All three have to join in. The father and mother together start the baby's body and God starts the baby's aliveness, gives it a soul, makes it a person, has a special idea of all the baby's abilities that it will ever reach right from the beginning.

How frightening that men have now decided to bypass this body involvement of husband and wife to manufacture a baby in a laboratory like a living puppet!

It is ironic that the only voice raised in defense of sex as the indispensable source of babies is the voice of the ascetical and supposedly antisex Pope Pius XII! He said:

> The child is the fruit of the marriage union, when it finds full expression by the placing in action of the functional organs, of the sensible emotions thereto related, and of the spiritual and disinterested love which animates such a union; it is in the unity of this human act that there must be considered the biological conditions of procreation. Never is it permitted to separate these different aspects to the point of excluding positively either the intention of procreation or the conjugal relation (Pius XII, "Allocution to the Second World Congress on Fertility and Sterility," May 19, 1956).

In modern language the Pope told this congress of human veterinarians, that the human child must be conceived of a sexual act between a man and a woman which is at once *fun, passionately* loving, unconditionally *giving,* and *open* to the possibility of conceiving! And that it is equally immoral to prevent a child by marital contraception or to have the child without mutual sexual surrender in a bodily way! The laboratory may not be substituted for the bedroom, the lab table for the marital bed! Excuse — the syringe for the penis!

Start Of The Baby

There is a special substance within the body of the mother and a substance in the body of the father, which when they meet together start the body of a baby, which is not a part of either of them, but is from the both of them together. There is an Hawaiian love song which a father sings to his baby, "Sweet Leilani, heavenly flower, nature fashioned you of roses wet with dew, and then she laid them in a bower. That was the start of you. Sweet Leilani, heavenly flower, I dreamed of Paradise for two, you are my paradise completed, you are my dream come true." A baby, then, is the *dream of love* between a mother and a father *come true*. The stuff in the father's body that helps make a baby is called the seed, though it is not like the seed which you see in an apple. The stuff in the mother's body is called the egg, though it is not like the egg that we put on the breakfast table. Both are unbelievably small and you really ordinarily do not see them at all.

How do the two get together in her body? It takes a very special kind of private, deep, intimate, enthusiastic love in which mother and father become two-in-one-flesh. The father has a part of his body like a tube, and when in love, he inserts this tube into the opening in the center of the mother's body. The father's seed passes through this tube into the mother's opening and keeps on going until it comes to the womb where it can meet the mother's egg and possibly form a new child. When God goes along with this activity, He gives a living soul to this bodily union of a cell from the mother's body and a cell from the father's body.

Every human being should get his or her start in the world in this way. But there was an exception for Jesus. Though Jesus lived in the little room in the body of his mother, called her womb, only Mary helped God make Jesus' body, no human father, helped God do this. St. Joseph was Mary's real husband but just Jesus' foster father who cared for Mary and for Jesus. Mary was and is a virgin. A virgin is a woman who has not had the experience of opening herself to a man sexually.

God has given you your being and your dad and I have cooperated with him in starting you off. You started in love. God loved you, your dad and I loved each other so that you were our love come true. Now you are called to give the gift of love back. You already know how much we want you to love us. But we want you to love God even more. You therefore want to give yourself, body and soul, back to God.

There are three ways of doing this. You want to save your body/soul gift and give it back to God in one of three different ways, and these are called *vocations* in life. God calls you into being through us and that call ought to be answered. That is why you have your own Christian name given in Baptism. You can answer it by giving yourself to Him directly and completely. This is the vocation of complete virginity which you see in the example of a nun, or a priest, or religious.

Marriage

You can give this bodily gift of yourself, when the time comes, to somebody who will be your husband or wife so that you can say to him or her that you are giving a gift which has never before been given to anybody but this husband or wife. You want him or her to take that gift and transfer it further to the God who tells you that this is a holy way of life called matrimony or marriage. Since this virginal gift, never before given to anybody else, needs a special person to receive or give it, you must try to grow in love until such time as you find the correct person through whom to give your virginal gift to God. It makes sense to pray that you will find a partner, if God calls you to marriage, who will help you to get to God through him or her and to fulfill God's plan for you. You must also pray that you will be the kind of person who will not prevent your partner from getting to God, but help him to do so. How terrible if you should be betrayed or betray your spouse in the name of LOVE!

Virginity In The World

Sometimes God does not seem to call a person to absolute virginity, leaving the call to marriage apparently open. But then He seems not to send along a suitable partner, perhaps for a long time, or for a whole lifetime. This might be the sign that God wants the individual to live in a single state of virginity, working in the world. There are many men and women who have recognized this call of God and become very devoted virile and feminine personalities who do not take the vows of religion, nor the vows of matrimony. It is wrong and cruel that the world sometimes laughs at them as though they were dried up and narrow persons and calls them bachelors (irresponsible men) and old maids (dried up, sour, unloving women).

It is important then, to bring a virginal body, a virginal self to God directly, or to God through a marriage partner. But this is quite difficult. Adam and Eve had no problem in controlling their natural desire for the love union before their Fall, but after they decided to make up their own rules for living, they found it extremely difficult. Scripture says that before the fall, they were naked and unashamed, but after the fall, they had to make clothing to cover themselves. Since the fall of Adam and Eve, you and I have trouble controlling this natural desire to have the bodily kind of union that opens itself to love and babies, and to keep such love expression within marriage. We are constantly tempted, once we are grown up or beginning to grow up, to have this experience without waiting for, or outside of, marriage. To have it this way would be evil and a sin.

What's This New Experience In My Body

It is important for parents to realize the possibility that a young child, particularly the boy, can experience spontaneous sexual arousal with apparently no external cause, though this is frequently not remembered by the individual. The little boy in particular is always disturbed by it, made uncomfortable, feels, somehow or other, that he ought not to be experiencing this. Nevertheless, when he attempts some kind of accommodation to the experience by touch, changing his position, rearranging clothing, he experiences some sort of pleasure for which there seems to be no explanation, and which unaccountably discomforts rather than satisfies him. Since the organ most directly connected with sexual pleasure in the female is hidden within the vagina, and is much smaller than the male penis, little girls are less likely to experience arousal, to attempt to sedate it by action, or to satisfy it by some sort of masturbatory action, though it is not unheard of that a girl discover and carry out masturbatory experience.

Often too, the boy's experience will be accompanied by fantasies or dreams not specifically sexual in their eroticism, but of some sort of tension, anxiety, fear, or even of excited anticipation, which has nothing to do with sex as such. In many cases, this early excitation totally disappears after a time (a year or so) and does not rise at all during the time we used to call the period of latency (from about 6 or 7 to 11 or 12). It returns at puberty, sometimes with sexual overtones, sometimes without.

If a parent observes the child in erection or masturbating, what ought he or she to do or say? Certainly the child should not be corrected harshly since there can be no question of sin at this time. The first thing is to make sure that clothing is reasonably loose. Tight shorts or panties should not generally be used for children for a number of reasons, for hygiene, good circulation, testicular development, as well as the possible arousal of tensions. Distractions can be provided to keep the child busy and interested and the child should be assured that there is nothing wrong with him or her, or in the reaction, that should concern them seriously. Perhaps nothing more need to be said, than that this happens to boys and girls in their growing up and that it is not generally a good idea to do anything more than take a comfortable position and to avoid the provision of pleasure. Just as the parent would try to prevent a child from scratching a mosquito bite, because it only makes the bite all the more red and itchy, so the parent ought to help the child avoid what is objectively, but not subjectively, a masturbatory action. If it seems wise, it might be enough to indicate that this kind of reaction will someday have meaning as one grows up to maturity, without any further analysis at that moment.

If this is all that ordinary, why should the parents do and say anything at all? Whether an activity is spontaneous or learned, when it is appropriated by the human person even in childhood, it sets up a pattern. A child who discovers sweets or salted foods, and who is constantly permitted and pacified by such foods, develops a physical habit which will eventually be harmful in its effects and make correct and healthful activities more and more difficult to interiorize. On the moral level, by analogy, one teaches the child early the difference between real truth and make-believe truth, lest permitting him to insist that a tiger ("the neighbor's cat") is in the back yard, gradually allows him to become a inveterate liar. In none of these cases, is the child capable of understanding why he itches, why he is attracted towards sweets, why it is he is tempted to fabricate, or why he experiences sexual stimulation. Nor is he capable of understanding why all of these things should be controlled, if not eliminated. Yet we correct all of them.

Immediately after the cessation of the possible tumescent and meaningless masturbatory experience of early childhood, boys and girls tend to enter a latency period in which they are strongly distanced from each other unless they are forced to be together. This should not be imposed. One wonders very much about co-educational class rooms during this period, but the "wisdom" of educators seems at this point insuperable. The Church has always been opposed to co-education in the sense of giving the same kind of formation to boys as to girls and she has not, officially at least, changed her mind on this topic. The period of early schooling is the period in which the process of sexual identity in an abstract way is achieved, but identity is learned just as effectively by contrast as by identification. Sufficient interaction between the sexes is usually provided in a houseful of children and visiting playmates. I do not discover white only by seeing white things, but also by contrasting them with black or other colors. I will never discover white if I see nothing but gray, or shades and tints, or if I never see black!

This does not mean that boys and girls cannot be friends. Friendship is the sharing of a common goal, interest, or pursuit. But the pursuit of femininity (identification) is obviously a friendship among girls and women, the pursuit of masculinity is a friendship among boys and men. Only when these come to friendship built upon the fullness which complementarity brings will there be cross sexual friendships, and only when *that* friendship is about the common good of family life (procreation-education of children) will the friendship of matrimony be formed — conjugal love.

Finally, in the thrilling context of the meaning of sexual intercourse indicated above in Chapter II, both the boy and the girl should be helped through the experience of sexual arousal with an awareness that this is a special gift of God to husbands and wives to lead them to follow the call of God into marriage and family, and to cooperate with Him in utter surrender to each other in a total gift of self and openness to the kind of living being called a human person who is unique, irrevocable, and gifted with a set of abilities to which all the world ought to remain open and helpful.

It should be clear from all the above that parental sex education will be different for each mother and father and for each child. Since persons are unique and defy stereotypes there can be no universally correct method of chastity education. In this matter, as in all loving interpersonal relations, *muddling through* is best!

Afterword

This book is not finished. It simply stops here! It does not conclude to anything. It merely opens up a lifetime of child parent interaction, of boy girl interrelating, of celibate and virginal meditation, of husband and wife maturation, of father mother growth — of discovering the delight that man and woman are different, correlative, polar, complementary, and that everyone is called to a nuptial union with God, directly or through another human being of correlative sex.

Sex education as chastity formation is never finished. One never fully understands what it is to be a person, to be a man, to be a woman, to be a father, to be a mother, to be a priest, to be a celibate or virgin, to be a single person who is happy to be so. I am a mystery to myself, and since sexuality is an inherent aspect of that mystery, so is sexuality a mystery. I am indefinite to the point of infinity. My life opens out invitingly to ever new experiences, or more importantly, to ever more *deep* experiences. But I do not have to travel to collect experiences, or meet many people, or have many sexual partners. I can spend a lifetime in exploring myself or you in love. I can surrender my sexual gift to God directly or though another person, and the surrender will go on, open-ended, forever.

I hope to spend an eternity unfolding endlessly ever new depths of love for myself, for you, and for God. I think, that though there will not be marriage in heaven because there will be no need to increase the human race, there will be repeated delightful discussions on love, masculinity, femininity, and nuptial love. Which was the greater nuptial lover? The ethereally simple virgin, St. Therese of Lisieux? Or the sorrowful prostitute Mary Magdalen who abjectly bathed the feet of Jesus with her tears and dried them with her hair, and was told that her many sexual sins were forgiven because she had loved deeply (Lk 7:47)? I can't wait to hear that sort of eternal debate.

Can you?

Sex Education In Schools — In General

The function of the school, the school room, and the teacher is primarily to inform the mind, and only secondarily to form the will, change emotional attitudes, persuade towards moral activity, inculcate public or private duty. The school is designed to teach *about* reality. It is a method of informing the mind with scientific knowledge whether that scientific knowledge is biology, mathematics, or even philosophy and ethics. Biology may teach that the living human organism is identified as having 46 chromosomes, that male and female are identifiable as having XX or XY chromosomes, that a fertilized ovum is a new individual human body, and not the body of the ovum producer or the sperm producer. The value of such an organism is not teachable by biologists, but only by an ethicist, philosopher or theologian. A political scientist can show that our founders indicated that all men are created equal with inalienable rights. But an attitude of respect, reverence and hands-off of human life can only be caught from parents, teachers and leaders who are themselves in awe of human life, and are not enamoured of absolute and unconditioned freedom of choice.

Value

A value is a good which is worth someone's while. We indicate that things are valuable when we are willing to take time and effort to obtain them, to spend ourselves, or income, in reaching out to them while sacrificing less important realities (either omitting the pursuit of them or even destroying them), and to defend them against loss or attack. We value our lives by taking time and effort to fulfill living potential, to remedy undeveloped abilities, and to defend our lives and the lives of other persons. We value our friends by cultivating their welfare. We value trust by trying to confide with confidence, and to be trustworthy for others. We value virginity if we believe that sexual love is only good when shared with but one other of opposite gender for a life-time open to a family of children.

Certain goods *ought* to be valued by *everyone*. For example, life and liberty are called inalienable rights by our Declaration of Independence. This means that these goods may be neither surrendered by the self nor destroyed or attacked from outside that self!

Other goods are valuable because we choose to make this one worth more of our efforts than that one. I might *prefer* to study philosophy rather than music; electronic physics rather than chemistry; prefer golf to tennis. These are the so-called private or merely personal values.

Generally, a public school pretends to give value-free education, or, at most, to talk *about* values and most often attempts to leave both intrinsic or arbitrary values up to the student, or to other agencies of formation (family, church, etc.) We say: "Diff'rent strokes for diff'rent folks!" And yet, the public cannot help but demand respect for certain existence and actions: good order, taking turns, being fair, telling the truth, honesty in homework, human life, personal property, etc.

At most, the public school might attempt to inculcate a sort of civic religion: observance of civic holidays, pledges of allegiance to the flag; respect for public laws and rules; politeness; memorization with awe of certain documents such as the Declaration of Independence; discussion of racism, etc. But apparently in our day, no civic responsibility or order is involved in "life-styles" whether religious, family, dietary, customary, sexual, et al. Strange. Our schools are being asked to solve the problems of drug addiction, epidemiological disease, juvenile and criminal delinquency, educational drop-out, unpreprogrammed pregnancy, family disintegration, racism, sexism (whatever that might mean), tax evasion, poverty, bigotry, etc., etc., while being forbidden to even describe or define religion, theism, justice, chastity, sexual modesty, honesty, industry, responsibility, commitment, and so on. No one seems to recall the dictum: "If there is no god, all things are allowed."

Virtue

A virtue is a regular and habitual choice of a good that is *truly* fulfilling of a human being. Sobriety is the habitual choice of being wide-eyed, alert and open to clearheaded thinking and choosing. Despite the fact that sobriety is often depicted as dull and boring, one has only to recall one's experience with some slobbering drunkard, or one's own desperate effort to recall whether one has made a fool of himself under the influence of alcohol, drugs, or marijuana, to realize that insobriety, drunkenness, hallucinatory intoxication are destructive of humanness and personhood.

The school can teach *about* the pursuit of the truly good, but it cannot effectively inculcate virtue because virtue is exemplified rather than defined and analyzed. It is caught rather than taught about. A medieval mystic once said it felicitously, "I had rather experience love than be able to define it." Despite this truth, there is the necessity for rational definition and analysis to provide the litmus test or the yardstick — the norm of judgment — for the existence of a virtue.

Since virtue is exemplified more effectively than it can be taught about, a virtue can be modeled by a teacher and projected to his pupils, but the pupil must also be on the teacher's wave length to perceive the virtue exemplified. It is the rare teacher who is so inspiring a person as to inspire an entire class. He or she is a superior teacher who can "turn on" 1/3 of the class, "turn off" another 1/3 and leave a final 1/3 merely indifferent. Jesus Christ Himself was unable to win a major number of His hearers to become disciples, and complains strongly of the indifferent. "I would that you were either hot or cold but because you are lukewarm, I will spew you out of my mouth" (Rev 3:16).

Not only do the teachers have different impact upon individual students, but frequently different teachers inspire different groups of students and no one can predict the impact beforehand. One can teach the truth in a scientific fashion and can demand and receive the necessary intellectual assent, but when one teaches about civic, personal, familiar or religious virtue, one experiences the old adage, "You can lead the horse to water, but you cannot make him drink." The identically good teacher might inspire one student and disgust another! An "evil" teacher can possibly inspire towards criminality or by antipathy towards virtue! Fagin in *Oliver Twist* taught little boys: "You've Gotta Pick a Pocket 'r Two!"

Certain kinds of topics have a special problem in being taught in a classroom. Any sort of vivid presentation has the tendency to evoke either strong appetite toward, or utter revulsion from the subject matter. This should need no proof, since we clearly use our media as a method of selling products (we call it advertising), and to promote or reject programs that we consider desirable or reprehensible. The Vietnam War was made violently unpopular by TV coverage in bloody color! The very same pictures might have been used to stir patriotism, forgiveness, justice, or diabolical vengeance!

Rhetoric is a sub-science in linguistics which analyses how to make ideas persuasive or repellent, and since a picture is worth a thousand words, we now have a "science" of marketing and advertising (a sort of pictorial rhetoric).

"Sex Education" In Public Schools?

Should there be a sex education program in our public and private nonsectarian schools on the primary and secondary school level? Should there be sex education in our social and cultural life? It depends on what one means by *sex education*! If one means that society and the school should understand and state that there are true differences in person, body, psychology, role, function, meaning, and significance between the sexes, then all human beings in their social interaction in and out of the classroom are engaged in sex education when they put ribbons in little girls' hair. We have distinct bath rooms for men and women. We used to engage in sex education when we had separate entrances to schools for boys and girls, and separate sex classrooms taught by teachers of their own sex, when men dressed in trousers and women in dresses. We engaged in sex education when we refused to teach formal courses on sexual anatomy and physiology, as well as on methods of sexual arousal, by implying that this was an intimate and private awareness to be absorbed directly or indirectly from parents, or from other agencies outside the school.

We engage in sex education today when we deny sexual differences, protest all cultural differences between men and women as an unjust "sexism." We have a reverse sort of sex education focussed upon interchangeable sexualness, or at least the mutuality of the sexes in classrooms of both sexes. For good or ill, we are allowing sex education of one sort or its opposite when we advance or retard the attempt to remove inclusive or supposedly "sexist" language from speech, journals or literature, or to prevent such removal. The revision of the Bible, Shakespeare, and classical literature in general to remove its witness to sexual differences in the culture of the past seems a very strong effort to *re-form* the sexes to unisex — which seems an oxymoron.

The above kinds of sex formation, however, are arguable from many sides in the public forum, in and out of the classroom situation. Sooner or later, there must be a consensus on this arrived at from a common philosophy of life and the sexes. One cannot successfully permit a community to be complacent that contradictory positions on sexualness can each be correct in that community. Either men and women are mathematically, psychologically, physically, functionally and interchangeably equal — identical — or they are not. Though generic sex formation of one kind or another cannot be eliminated from any human interaction, and certainly obtains in all classrooms whether consciously or not, something further is usually meant by "sex education in the schools." This term no longer suggests proportionate references to reproduction in the biology classroom; to bodily hygiene in the health courses; to family and social customs in sociology, anthropology, geography and social studies; to chastity and modesty, or marital commitment in the discussion of ethical or legal matters; etc.

Today, sex education seems to refer to the formal teaching of a science of *sexology*, the study of the various ways in which people live and achieve the physiological experiences of tumescence and orgasm either alone or with others, together with the results of such activity, whether of venereal disease, permanent or temporary living arrangements with one's own or the opposite sex, the pursuit, prevention, reversal or acceptance of pregnancy, the transfer of venereal diseases, in a completely amoral (or unmoral) context.

Our schools do not teach about all the methods of making noises with vocal chords: of communication by speech; various processes of information and disinformation, love and hate, praise and insult, politeness and vulgarity, persuasion to good and seduction to evil; patriotism or betrayal — in an amoral context! We implicitly teach either honesty or dishonesty in speech. Truth always or emergency lying!

Such science of sexology, however necessary it might be for a professional physician or counselor, has no place in the school system for children or adolescents. One questions the wisdom of such courses on "Human Sexuality" as are taught even in colleges. One does not teach obstetrics in an ordinary human physiology course, even on the college level! One does not teach bank-vault-exploding techniques in Criminal Justice! A formal course in *sexology* is utterly disproportionate within the various scientific and sociohistorical disciplines that ought to be taught on the primary and secondary level.

A further reason, however, is involved in the fact that science is supposedly objective and attempts to be descriptive rather than normative. It implies that no norms should be proposed to the student. One need not talk about atomic war when speaking of atomic physics. On the college level, it is suggested that the norms ought to be discovered in courses on philosophical (or religious studies) ethics. In high schools it is suggested that it ought to be left to courses on religion and since it is forbidden to teach any religion (or even *about* religions!) in the public schools, this should be absorbed completely and only from parents and religious leaders.

But "value-free" science is a myth! Even in his choice of objects of research and its methods, the scientist reveals his conscious or unconscious moral bias. The "science" of Kinsey and Margaret Mead, as well as of Freud, have been attacked as dishonestly biased.

Values' Clarification

Frequently the analysis of such norms is left to a vague course of "Values Clarification." In such courses students are merely asked to propose their own value system to others and listen respectfully to the value system of their peers. It is suggested that neither they nor their teachers ought to promote or inculcate their own value system and ought not to be judgmental of the value systems of others. Though this sounds delightfully nonmoralizing, as a matter of fact it proposes to the students a complete indifferentism to all values, and urges them simply to accept "diff'rent strokes for diff'rent folks." Indifferentism is itself a value system! Toleration becomes the only absolute, which demands that a *non-absolute* is the absolute! An oxymoron! That *choosing* (pro-choice) itself is what alone *makes* the chosen reality to be good, desirable, valuable!

As a matter of objective fact, however, **Values' Clarification** seems to be hostile to any strongly held traditional sexual values. If tolerance of contradictory values is an absolute, then one must be intolerant of, hostile to, any choice of one to the rejection of another! Sex Education as Sexology must be hostile to anyone holding in favor of chastity, modesty, privacy, premarital virginity, heterosexuality, inviolability of sexual intercourse and of the conceptive result, and opposing marital contraception, abortion, fornication, adultery, masturbation, pederasty, sodomy, pornography, *et al.*

Sex education as sexology appears to have strong values' inculcation! It clearly considers orgasm a positive health entity and orgastic or coital abstinence neither desirable nor probable — or even possible! It suggests that no method of orgastic release is preferable to any other, and therefore no method should be arguable or argued! Orgastic release is suggested as birthright from the moment of possible tumescence (even in utero!).

Yet, sexological sex education has apparently been assigned the obligation of preventing what most persons have become convinced are incidentally undesirable consequences of otherwise good activities. Orgastic activity must be made to be "safe" from extraneous and harmful consequences. The inculcation of "Safe Sex" is a required value assignment. Orgasm and coitus must be "protected" against commitment to another person, any or every venereal disease, unpreprogrammed pregnancy. Every means to protect libido against, or reverse (breaking-up, divorce, antibiotics, spermicides, morning after drugs, abortion on demand, infanticide of the defective) these dangers become a value to be urged!

Strange, after early pro-choice publicity for smoking and euphoric drugs, one no longer hears urging for filter cigarettes, and the provision of sterile needles. "Say **No** to smoking! Say **No** to (recreational) drugs!" Our schools do not seem able to use the parental slogan: "Say **No** to insignificant and inconsequential orgasm (Extramarital and sterilized coitus)!

Libido Eros

A further problem on all levels is that the study of sexology is inherently stimulative for all normal human males and females. It is simply absurd for anyone, who analyzes his or her own response to the TV screen and to the kind of movies available, to suggest that classroom study of sexology can be without sexual arousal of the students. This is even true for those who can claim the necessity for such scientific study in order to become professional counselors, physicians, psychiatrists, etc. That therapists have been notorious for seducing or being seduced by their patients, or even by the subject matter, is easily proven from journalistic and scientific studies. The psychoanalytic couch has not always been exclusively used for the free association of *ideas*! Failures (addictive masturbation, pedophilia, pederasty, incest, Lolita complexes, mutual seduction, fornications, etc.) by professionals (clergy, religious, teachers, lawyers, psychologists, psychiatrists, physicians, therapists, lay therapists, even parents and siblings) fill the pages of "scandal" sheets, to the pharisaical scandal of all, while contradictorily providing arguments against celibacy, monogamy, fidelity, marital indissolubility, heterosexuality, premarital chastity, modesty of dress and eyes. (The argument: if so many fail to achieve these values, either generally or even perfectly, the moral sexual norm ought to be reversed to measure up to practice, pessimistic realism; i.e., "If I am not near the girl I love, I love the girl I'm near!")

It is strange that for drug-and-alcohol addiction education programs, one does not merely present the impact of intoxication upon the nervous system and the euphoric results, together with some consideration of possible "side effects," nor do such programs suggest that the student ought to be free to select whatever results he would prefer to achieve. Nor do we teach nutrition from a "values clarification" point of view. Further, we do not teach the various methods of bringing about bodily harm and death and allow the students to make up their minds about violence. We clearly understand that even the vivid picture of violence is contraindicated as is proven by our recent concern with the excess of violence and its too vivid portrayal upon the TV screen. Our more and more frequent discovery of pornography as the stimulus to incest and child abuse indicates that such approaches should not be permitted in a classroom.

Does this mean that there should be no sex education in a classroom? If the definition of sex education is restricted to the areas of sexology already indicated, it is quite clear that sexology should not be taught on any level, other than in the graduate training of professionals for whom such detailed information might be necessary or helpful, with whatever proportionate risk to their own moral integrity. However, if sex education involves the presentation of various other disciplines in which references to sexual differences and genital activity are properly to be found, a whole new set of norms would seem to be applicable.

Generally speaking, to whatever level in a particular discipline other aspects are presented, to that level references to sexual differences and sexual practice are proper. For example, the study of nutrition on any

level might be paralleled by the study of reproduction with similar peda-
gogical techniques. One should not teach biology as though there were no
reproductive system! But quite obviously just as the study of nutrition
does not demand a trip to the bathroom in order to analyze the physiology
of defecation, or a discussion of the liturgy of bathroom practice, and
vulgar language, so an awareness of the reproductive system does not
need a trip to the male or female restrooms to observe the different
generative plumbing systems of boy and girl! Or the use of obscene
language.

Whose Values?

If one accepts that it is impossible to teach facts without inculcating
desirability or undesirability for the activities involved, the problem of
schooling in a pluralistic society is serious to the point of impossibility.
Pluralism means that a number of ultimately irreconcilable value systems
are publicly and socially interchangeable in a society. There will be no
problem for a pluralism of mere taste differences. One can teach good
nutrition without discussing differences in generic cuisine, or suggesting
that one is superior to the other. But one cannot merely propose pro-
choice for meat eaters, if one denies superior rights for humans (insists
that speciesism is equivalent to racism), unless he also permits cannibalism! Nor can he allow the public discussion of obligatory vegetarianism
versus the permissibility of human cannibalism.

In classroom discussion of sexual behavior in modern life, if one
considers such behavior as *merely* private (diff'rent strokes for diff'rent
folks), there ought to be no public discussion! If sexology merely details
human private behavior of no social or public value, it ought not to be a
scientific discipline for a public discussion. It belongs only in the interpersonal interaction of family and religious membership.

If it is insisted that there ought to be public teaching of attitudes in
these areas, then each value-group has the right to form its own members
toward its own value system. Nor is it sufficient, in compulsory public
schooling, merely to excuse any one or other group from exposure to the
value system of a majority. Our Supreme Court has declared that the
excusing of any objectors from public religious practice, no matter how
apparently ecumenical, discriminates unjustly against those excused by
stigmatizing them as different from the others. If this is valid then similar

excusing of religious children from secularistic "sex education" is equally discriminating against them. No. Either separate education according to the values of their parents must be provided in parallel time and intensity, or no such education must be permitted. At the very least equal time and intensity might be provided for comparative consideration and rhetorical support for every competing value system. Yet, since children and adolescents are hardly considered capable of choosing, for example, sobriety over drug euphoria while still under the control of their parents, no such value choices should be presented.

All the disciplines on the primary and secondary level will have some reference to the differences between the sexes, and the way in which people live their sexual lives. History, geography, literature, biology, sociology, all will have some references and the reasonable references should not be interdicted or excluded from the presentations. Hamlet cannot be discussed without some knowledge of affinitive incest and marital *crimen.* Hawthorn's *Scarlet Letter* cannot be read without knowing that Adultery is what is referred to in the novel by the Puritan demand that the sinner wear the Scarlet "A" on her clothing. (Curious, Might modern teenage peers demand that the Scarlet "A" refer to Abstinent?) Can the study of history somehow provide an analysis of the Christian West without presenting its value system?

Secular Humanism

A problem arises here in that a more and more conscious or unconscious secular humanism has become, or is rapidly becoming, the public philosophy. This philosophy presents an indifferentism to any objective values in which each individual human person becomes his own norm for value choices. It must be further understood that today a philosophy of life is being taught more explicitly by the selection of literature and films than by any formal program in philosophy, ethics or religion! What one reads or views as literature or art is often presented without any objective and inherently desirable set of values.

Secular humanism insists that human beings alone exist at the pinnacle of being, that there is no God who creates reality or a significant universe, that there is no rhyme or reason to be implemented or destroyed by free choice, and that there is no after life or judgment, approval or retribution. That alone is morally good for an individual which he chooses as an option in preference to either its contradictory or its contrary. All decisions are merely arbitrary options, each interchangeably desirable as its opposite! To preserve one's life is interchangeably desirable with suicide. To preprogram a child in a test-tube (with or without previously known gametes) is interchangeably moral with killing one already started.

It would seem that some sort of public philosophy in the area of sexual experiencing might be agreed upon as for the public good. At minimum, one would suppose that our historical norm should be continued at least in theory if not always in practice: monogamous marriage between two persons of opposite sex eventuating in a family of own or adopted children, with the restriction of sexual practice to a publicly recognized state called matrimony. This obviously should be the normative ideal for all and should be presented to children and adolescents for their pursuit. In this view, divorce, extramarital and premarital sex are clearly socially undesirable realities. Since children should be born and raised within a stable marital family, sexual activity ought to be initiated only in such a situation as to be able to welcome the advent and nurturance of the child.

To suggest that difficult marriages ought to be solved by divorce and unprogrammed pregnancies ought to be remedied by contraception or abortion is to suggest that sexual experience is desirable as a healthy entity at all costs, and that less than happy events, whether of commitment, pregnancy, or venereal disease ought to be antecedently prevented by experimental testing out or by contraceptive or contrainfectious practice. Consequent complications should be remedied by divorce, abortifacients, or antibiotics.

No such public philosophical consensus on sexuality seems to exist, at least so far as our elite leaders are concerned, whether in education, journalism, literature, politics, law, medicine, therapy, the media, art, academia, or even liberal religion, despite the fact that the majority of the populace pursues these sexual values, if not always in the observance, at least in admittedly guilty breach! Heterosexual lifetime fidelity as foundation of a family of children is still the ideal. Brides would still like white to be significant. Even soap operas celebrate the sexual wilderness with tears!

An educational and media elite cannot be permitted to select the moral value system for the majority, any more than generals can be allowed to impose whatever is their own elite morality of war.

Coeducation

One of the major problems facing us today, is the problem of sexual identification, the discovery of and self-identification with some set of norms for masculinity and femininity.

All knowledge is founded upon the two principles of identity and contradiction. A certain reality is what it is and no other than it is. When there are various manifestations of the same universal reality, the reality itself is identified by repeated comparisons with concrete examples of the same nature. The human being in experiencing various things that can be called white eventually come to understand that white is white, is white, is white.

But that same person learns that all other colored reality is contradictory or contrary to white. A child then learns that white is not black, nor any color but white. He learns from the principle of contradiction as well as by the principle of identity.

If boys are not girls and girls not boys, men not women, and women not men, then appreciation of one's sex is a process of multiple comparison, identification, and contrast and distancing, with multiple examples and models.

The Catholic Church has always been opposed to coeducation in the sense of treating boys and girls in identical fashion, giving them identical formation and information assigning identical roles in living. Such education would imply the interchangeability of the sexes, instead of their equality in correlative value, and alternating superiority one to the other in a kaleidoscope of mutuality. Unisex in education blurs the edges of the principles of identity and contradiction, and as a result it makes it more difficult to achieve sexual identification, the number one psychological hurdle today.

Our attempts to remove all examples of virility versus femininity in our school textbooks, does not eliminate stereotypes, it merely destroys any role playing which is characteristically masculine or feminine, and tries to model "unisex" which is, even in the word, absurd! (*Sex* is division, *oneness* the denial of division!)

A stereotype is a perfectly repeated casting of a printing plate from a paper-maché mold. Examples of masculinity or femininity upon which the observer is asked to model himself or herself and to appropriate in one's unique fashion is not stereotyping. A boy should have as many loved role models of masculinity as can possibly be presented to him in his father, a favorite uncle, a boy-scout leader, a basketball coach, an inspiring teacher, an older brother and buddies who shape and share his dreams of masculine prowess. He should also have as many as possible models of femininity and motherliness from which to draw and build a composite picture of how he will contrast with and someday relate to girlfriends, his fiancée, his wife, womanly coworkers, the mother of his children, etc. Of course, this is also correlatively true of the young woman, who may need fewer models but more closely loved ones. The success of all romantic fairy tales, movies and literature depends upon the imaginative portrayals of concrete personages. To be a person is not a neuter self-achievement of such uniqueness as to have no imitation involved. Persons are not absolutely unique but always masculine or feminine persons, not a mixture of each in an androgynous fashion. It is simply not true that "there are no differences between the sexes except the accidental differences of their generative apparatus."

Coeducation in the same classrooms is particularly difficult in the prepuberty and early puberty years. Generally speaking, boys are as much as two years behind girls in physical and emotional maturation. Girls have greater attention span than do boys and develop verbal skills earlier and more thoroughly. Early classroom competition tends to favor the girls over the boys. More often than not, the girls are anxious to please than are boys. It doesn't take much by way of observation to note that boys and girls react quite differently to the various kinds of approval and affirmation given by the teacher, and especially to correction, disapproval and/or punishment.

Our modern tendency is to demand fairness, which is identical treatment for the same behavior and achievement. It is difficult (practically impossible) to be *fair* in a classroom of boys and girls who show such basic differences. It is even more difficult, if not impossible, to give identical treatment to *unique* differences within and between the sexes.

What is to be done where coeducation in the same classroom has already become universally accepted? I think the following norms should be included.

Boys and girls should be treated with some external differences within the same classroom and should be expected to deal with each other in a manner which emphasizes some correlatively between the sexes, rather than either identity or rivalry. Generally speaking, boys should not be in competition as a group with the girls so that one sex seems superior or inferior to the other. If rivalry does happen it should be directed toward correlative strengths, rather than either/or. Individual boys should rival other boys and individual girls should rival other girls, lest competition should become antithetical rather than correlative.

In the earlier school years it would seem that a maximum number of teachers should or could be women, since children of both sexes need strong relationships to a mother and mother figures. However as the time of oedipal crossover approaches it is imperative that more and more masculine teachers be presented to the boys as role models, and quite possibly as contrasting figures of virility for the girls. Of dubious value are teachers who specialize in the single subject (or two) for a multiple number of students. In the name of efficiency and competence, often enough the interpersonal relationship with fewer students at a time is sacrificed. Since, as already said, masculinity and femininity is more easily caught than taught, few good models closely observed at greater length and imitated would seem to be preferable to many more casual and ephemeral contacts.

A primary difficulty in modern education is the possible and probable identification with a loved and respected teacher who might nevertheless provide harmful points of identity and contrast. In the formative years of primary and secondary schooling, teachers in the process of falling in love, marrying, divorcing, and remarrying cannot help but have impact for good or ill upon their students. Their experiences may not affect the professionalization of mathematics, for example, but will surely influence observant students from whom the facts of impact upon their lives clearly cannot be withheld. Of serious impact is the pregnant and unwed teacher, practicing homosexuals and lesbians, and the multiple teachers who insist that they have every right to explain, defend and promote their own life-styles (possibly unacceptable to society). It is well known that even child abusers or terrorist kidnappers gain and frequently retain the love and respect of those that they have even abused, or terrorized!

A problem which faces every teacher, man or woman, in a Catholic or public school is the problem of romantic falling in love by a pupil and the temptation to reciprocate (called transference and countertransference).

Even the youngest of children can have a passionate crush upon a teacher of either sex. This is not usually a situation involving bodily sexuality, but its potential for disaster is always there. It is the wise teacher who knows how to accept kindly the romantic love offer and disengage himself or herself from it without trauma to the child. It is the even wiser teacher who provides the chaperonage of time, place and situation which will make any untoward activity less likely or less tempting. It is the most wise principal or parent who is alert to the possibilities without being fearsomely suspicious. If this seems an unusual caution, one has only to look over the titles of movies now being made available in theatres and in videotapes such as *Private Lessons, Homework,* etc., in which teachers are depicted as initiating students into orgastic and coital activities.

The greatest difficulty with coeducation is in the teaching of sexual practices in the presence of such great sexual differences among pubescent boys and girls.

First. There is the problem of latency. According to the majority of psychologists there is a period of latency in sexual interest for both boys and girls in which an earlier interest in sexual difference fades into disinterest to the point of hostility! In the process of sexual identification, strong embrace of one's own masculinity or femininity tends to flight from the opposite. The nursery rhyme indicates this: "What are little boys made of? Ships and snails, and puppy dog tails, that's what little boys are made of. What are little girls made of? Sugar and spice, and everything nice, that's what little girls are made of." It would seem that the period of latency is a period of consolidation of sexual identity, and should not be invaded or attacked. It seems that the proponents of formal sex education in the schools are determined to deny that such a period of latency exists, and to invade it at all costs. It is impossible not to invade latency in the junior high school, since estrogen surges in girls almost two years sooner than does testosterone in boys. Girls are attracted to boys several years older than those in their own junior high classroom. Boys are not attracted, in the beginning, to any girls in their own class, except perhaps as asexual buddies, and hardly to any girls older or younger than themselves.

Second. The advent of puberty for boys and girls is not only separated by at least two years on the average, but the physiological, emotional and adjustment problems are vastly different. The experience of ovulation and menarche for girls and of tumescence without apparent external stimulus and nocturnal emission for boys are not of immediate interest and concern for the opposite sex, and are too personal an experience to be shared in groups, or even discussed with equanimity.

Third. At different hormonal and psychological levels between the two sexes in general, and among varying individual growth in particular, it is practically impossible to have classroom description and discussion of genital activities without tumultuous psychological and stimulative reaction. It seems impossible that a description of "Safety" and "Sex" as "Safe Sex" be presented without unjustified sexual stimulus in boys (masturbatory) and an ambivalent attraction-repulsion in girls.

Nor does it seem possible for coeducative higher grades. Surely, if one considers "personal" values to be one's own individual values, such should be inculcated on a one-to-one individually personal level. This is obviously a parental role. That parents might find it difficult to perform their duty is rather an argument against others doing it, than for classroom education! Parents instinctively shrink from having their own privacy invaded and invading the privacy of children. Teachers must be even more hesitant!

The Goal Of Schooling

The goal of schooling is the inculcation of those disciplines which will enable a person to free himself from ignorance and contribute to the overall common good. The most fundamental goal of schooling is literacy which is the ability to read, write and to communicate truth and goodness in speech. But literacy as a mere ability to decipher words is secondary to *what* one is enabled to read and how she or he absorbs it. An illiterate man was once convicted and sentenced for armed robbery. During his years of incarceration, he completed primary and secondary education and received a diploma. About a year after his release he was again back in prison, this time for forgery! He had learned to read, but he had read nothing which indicated his obligations to respect property and pursue a common good with his fellow citizens.

A second goal of schooling is to provide those *skills* necessary both for social living and for earning one's daily bread. But again these skills must be developed in some atmosphere of social responsibility. A skillful photographer can become an artist of the beautiful, an illustrator, a recorder of newsworthy events, an advertiser of worthy products or a pornographer. He will probably earn most monetary reward for the last! His value system? Pro-Choice?

A student of chemistry might be interested in pure research, discovering better detergents, inventing new antibiotics or producing "angel dust!" Is the last merely an optional life-style of great monetary "worth?"

Generally speaking, our public schools are concerned with providing the fundamental disciplines of literacy, and an introduction to the various scientific disciplines and also such virtues as will promote the civil common good. It is for these three goals that principals, teachers and school boards select the various curricula and teaching aids, as well as books in the library, which will forward these goals. Not every kind of knowledge, though apparently good in itself, is used wisely and well for one's own and another's good. One would be surprised and shocked to discover formal courses, and sections of the library, on methods of breaking into computer codes, revolutionary tactics, behavior modification by subliminal perception, "do it yourself" atomic bombs, for amateur production, or how to sell machine guns for experts. No, public schools try to select inspiring literature, history which indicates the wisdom of democratic government, honesty in business, the evil of intoxication and drug abuse, the obligation of voting and paying taxes in order to promote the common good.

Quite clearly our public school system should not teach sexology as a discipline which would be merely the presentation of all the methods of achieving sexual orgasm for either sex either alone or with others of one's own and *opposite* sex and the resulting consequences of such activity — venereal disease, pregnancy either in or out of wedlock, temporary commitment and uncommitment, etc., while allowing the students to view these things against their own unique and individual and contradictory value systems. This would be like teaching about atomic energy and its evocation by merely pointing out the power to be released and allowing the students to consider their own value systems in terms of the harvesting of energy or the releasing of it for any purpose they choose including the wiping out of innocent "enemies." The knowledge and ability to release atomic energy must be taught only in the context of its possible uses as a peacetime source of energy and perhaps of self-defense and reasonable deterrence of unjust aggression.

It is very interesting that SIECUS (Sex Information Education Council of the United States) proposes precisely the inculcation of sexology with an indifference to any particular value system in its regard. Further, this organization suggests very strongly to its followers that it introduce sexology courses into schools on all levels and that it withdraw its proposals only long enough to defuse opposition and then return again until its ideas are adopted. SIECUS and ASSECT (American Society of Sex Education Counselors and Therapists) are clearly dedicated to the proposal that orgasm is a health entity which should be encouraged in every individual from before his birth to the moment of death so that the number of orgasms and that the intensity thereof measure up to the desire of the person who chooses them. The only limit to such activity, it is suggested, is the willingness of any desirable partner to participate. Such willingness may depend upon the persuadability of the respondent and seems to demand only some sort of maturity. Generally this is phrased — "anything is permissible between consenting adults." But, according to recent legislation, a consenting adult is anyone who has reached puberty and wishes to respond freely to sexual approach. This is clearly indicated in a number of court decisions which teach that a child is sexually *emancipated* from his parents at the moment of puberty since he or she can obtain contraceptive and abortion information and service without the consent, control or knowledge of his or her parents.

Correct School Sex Education

In the public school system, the minimum that ought to be demanded is that sexual knowledge be inculcated, if at all, in a context of a civic virtue which will defend and promote the fundamental building block of civic society, which is the nuclear family of husband, wife and own or adopted children. It is quite clear that the common good of the American nation is being eroded by the disintergration of the nuclear family through pre- and extramarital promiscuity, divorce and remarriage, spouse and child abuse, rape and various sexual addictions, as well as by resultant disease and abandoned spouses and children.

It is important to note here a new, recent definition of the "extended family." In times gone by, an "extended family" was considered to be a clan — a group of nuclear families — linked, often by proximity, but more inclusively by blood relationships, in a common ancestry. The nuclear family's membership in a clan accepted some responsibility for all other families of the same clan and provided interest, concern, almsgiving, social welfare and care for their less than successful, needy or calamitous familial members. In the more mobile social situation of the United States, an "extended" family comprises those nuclear families which are headed by those who were brothers, sisters or cousins to each other and kept together in a network of communications, mutual interests, mutual services and regular gatherings and celebrations.

In recent times, however, the concept of "extended" family has changed remarkably and in revolutionary fashion. The idea is applied more recently to the network of divorced and remarried as well as mobile families. Today a child may be considered in an "extended" family because he has a natural father, a step father, a natural mother, a mother married to his natural father, one or more coterminous or successive father figures heading the household in which he lives and a whole congeries of blood and contractual relationships with the offspring of the various possible progenitors who come into and out of his life. It is also important to realize that there is a strong pressure to redefine family from its traditional meaning of one man married to one woman with their *own* children to mean a household of individuals who merely live together whether in a nuclear configuration or a communal or kaleidoscopic one (odd couples, homosexual arrangements, sexual communes, etc.). This restricts a family to any kind of shared living space, a household for any social life-style.

One would anticipate that the civic community has some sort of ideal in terms of family towards which its educational effort points. One would presume then, that the sex education in the context of social virtue, would indicate in the various disciplines those facts which would orient the students towards the civic virtue of family life and loyalty. This would suggest that biology be concerned with reproduction of animals in a veterinarian or "nature studies" sense and for human beings in orientation to human children and family life. One does not study the physiology of orgasm in animals. One need not study the physiology of orgasm in human beings. In social studies, the impact of a good sex education would imply the wisdom of the nuclear family, the concept of fidelity, loyalty and exclusivity, the desirability of chastity and modesty to preserve the integrity of the home. If such civic virtue cannot be a goal to be inculcated for all, then **No** sex education of any kind can be permitted in our public school system.

Sex Education In Catholic Schools and in CCD

Religious Education

Education in parochial or private schools of religious orientation is an attempt to integrate all of the educational process in the classrooms and suffuse every study with religious awareness. To write about chastity education in the context of a parochial school is to immerse oneself in the middle of things all at once. In the purely religious schools of education such as the traditional Confraternity of Christian Doctrine, the teacher must leave all the other disciplines to the public schools and concentrate exclusively upon religious content in the mere forty hours per year that he can have with his (often) reluctant pupils.

Writing is done in a progressive manner. Textbooks and lesson plans attempt to be logical and orderly, proceeding from *first* this, and *second* that, and so on, as also to imply that once the first step has been taken, it will never need to be repeated. Christian character formation, on the other hand, and sex formation into chastity and modesty in particular, does not proceed with logical order or temporal steps! Everything is grist for its mill at any time, in any order as well as in every course and step of knowledge. Every teaching effort is to be suffused with implicit or explicit Christian inspiration.

There are no suggested "lesson plans" in this part of the book. Parents should simply expect that the following material is the "ecology" of the Catholic educational effort within which chastity education is inculcated.

Another difficulty comes from the fact that the area of sexual formation, however oriented towards chastity, cannot be the focus of a subject in itself for two reasons.

First, sexualness as quality of person affects the child and the teacher in every respect of his or her being and cannot be abstracted from personhood for study without crippling the awareness of total personhood. The butterfly is killed when it is mounted in a specimen case and classified. Taxonomy (the classification tool that Kinsey used first to study wasps!) tells us the varieties of insects in entomology. But the butterfly is understood only in its natural habitat, and even then when it is not studied *exclusive* of all other interactive reality there. In some ways a half attentive child learns more about the butterfly on a lazy summer afternoon in a meadow than a taxonomist ever learns. Kinsey used taxonomy (physical classification on measured scale) on bodily sexuality to fraudulently found the sexual revolution. Kinsey founds the entire modern sexual revolution (the revolution which took orgasm out of marriage and made it insignificant and inconsequential) upon descriptions and numbering of meaningless sexual paroxysms and made them the norm of correctness! (cf. Reisman and Eichel, *Kinsey, Sex and Fraud, The Indoctrination of a People* [Lafayette, LA: Lochinvar-Huntington, 1990.])

Secondly, focus upon the sexual aspect of genitality is inherently and disproportionately stimulative of sexual arousal.

But all Christian education can be illustrated again and again from its impact upon human sexualness and sexuality and the characteristic masculinity and femininity of the student and teacher can illustrate divine revelation. Both their libido (sexual drive) and their eros (romantic thrills) influence their awareness of the realities discussed. (Cf. Concupiscence of the flesh and eyes, below.)

Mental Distinctions

The very distinction and separation of the topics below is in some ways self-defeating for adequate *Christian* sex-education. (Read **only** *chastity formation!*) Education is an immersing, not a didactic process.

Nor is any single area of special importance at any particular time in the child's level of education from Kindergarten to Grade 12. Some awareness of modesty, and matrimony, and sin, and paternal and maternal responsibility, and vocational considerations will be important in the Kindergarten and will be no less important in the 12th grade, college and old age!

Despite all this, an attempt will be made to indicate where, in the various disciplines, some impact can be made upon the formation of boys and girls to become men and women, who are celibate or virginal, while they are called in true vocational awareness towards the spousal gift of self directly and immediately to God in religious dedication or to a Christian spouse in Christ within the sacrament of matrimony.

There should be no such thing as a formal education in sexual practices in the Catholic School. Detailed description about sexual practices is inherently stimulative and suggestive for both teacher and students. Strictly speaking there should be no formal course called sex education at all. The education must always be towards chastity and modesty. Any description which is in itself stimulating to sexual arousal or towards illicit romantic love would be a sinful immodesty on the part of a teacher or student, unless the risk of such is necessary for the formation of the child or children. That is the reason this book is entitled "Challenging Children to Chastity." In a different, but no less important way, it would be bad pedagogy to assign even a classic story of vengeance for reading unless one also suggested the analysis of what is just punishment, what is sinful anger, what is vicious vendetta, and what is virtuous forgiveness.

Frequent and indirect references to the area of love, sex, marriage, family and Christian virtues should be introduced in every area of education in the Catholic school. But seldom if ever should there be a formal course on sexual practices as such, even in order to describe all the practices one must condemn as sins. St. Paul, though he teaches much about chastity, modesty, and inveighs against unchastity, in his analysis of vice says:

> Be imitators of God as his dear children. Follow the way of love, even as Christ loved you. He gave Himself for us as an offering to God, a gift of pleasing fragrance [all about positive goodness]. As for lewd conduct or promiscuousness or lust of any sort, let them not even be mentioned among you; your holiness forbids this. Nor should there be any obscene, silly, or suggestive talk; all this is out of place. . . . Make no mistake about this: no fornicator, no unclean or lustful person — in effect an idolater — has any inheritance in the Kingdom of Christ and of God. Let no one deceive you with worthless arguments. These are sins that bring God's wrath down upon the disobedient. Therefore have nothing to do with them (Eph 5:1-7 from New American Bible).

Only those sexual definitions should be taught which can, in an abstract fashion, define for the student what is being referred to. This will be apparent in what follows.

Salvation History

From the time the youngest child is taught the story of creation — of Adam and Eve; of the Fall; of Noah and his family in the Ark; Abraham, Moses, David and the chosen people; of Christmas as well as the life, death and resurrection of Jesus Christ as He established His Church; of the wedding feast prepared for us in heaven — through the time the older child or adolescent can be expected to read the scriptures profitably, many opportunities are presented to the teacher and to the child for the presentation of the Christian awareness of masculinity and femininity and the spousal meaning of the body. The Hail Mary, the story of the Annunciation, the trip of Mary to help in the delivery of Elizabeth (the Visitation), and Christmas provide all the opportunity a teacher might need to speak about virginity, the waiting for the command of God before entering into conjugal intimacy in marriage, the pro-life awareness that Jesus was incarnate in human flesh at the moment of the Annunciation, that pregnancy takes 9 months (Annunciation [March 25] to Christmas [December 25]), that Mary was present at the delivery of her nephew St. John the Baptist, that Jesus was born of a woman and nursed at her breasts — all this will demand that the very youngest child have some, however vague, awareness of the following definitions: virgin, carnal knowledge, ("I do not know man!" Lk 1:34), marriage as a commitment to consummate some sort of intimate union, womb and pregnancy, delivery, nursing, the love of man and women in marriage and God's involvement in it, the role of responsibilities for men and woman as indicated by the utter surrender of self-gift in Mary and the responsibility of Joseph for the welfare of the Holy Family.

Covenant Theology

Since the entire history of salvation involves an *Old* Testament or Covenant, and a *New* Testament or Covenant, and the two Covenants are between God and His chosen people and between Christ and His Church, one can hardly speak of Judaeo-Christian truth without focusing upon the meaning of a covenant which is a wedding of two distinct and disparate realities in spousal and family fashion.

The first and most important lesson that children must learn is that a covenant, which, in ancient times and usually between previously warring tribes, one strong, and the other weak, became a treaty of peace and was celebrated by marrying the more powerful chieftain's son to the less powerful chieftain's daughter so that both tribes would become blood relatives in their children. The marriage was celebrated by a sacrificial offering of some living animal to the deity, and the eating of the roasted flesh, so that the guests would become one flesh with each other (and with God!) in sharing the same life support from the meal and in recognizing their mutual willingness to die in defense of each other. A covenant is a mutual assumption of family loyalty and services, not a mere contract to provide things or services for a fee! Contracts can be voided. Covenants cannot! A boy *cannot* deny the fatherhood of his father, even though he is faithless to his teaching. A father *cannot* deny his orientation to his son, even though he might hate him murderously! And we all know that infanticide and patricide are despicable crimes for every culture! A covenantal treaty between nations swears to carry out this matrimonial, parental and filial relation among its signatories. Unconditional. Irreversible.

In the Old Testament, God repeatedly extends His Covenant ever further and further: to a *couple* with Adam and Eve; to a *family* with Noah; to a *tribe* with Abraham-Isaac; to a *nation* with Moses-Aaron; to a *kingdom* with David-Solomon; to *all mankind* through Jesus Christ. There is no doubt but that divine revelation fastens upon the "two in one flesh" of marriage for God's repeated offer and insistence upon marriage of divinity with humanity. Most of the prophets see the chosen people, however faithless and fickle they might be, as an unconditionally loved bride (cf. Hosea *passim*; Ezechiel 16). And the children of this union, even individually, find their value and significance resulting from this marital unity.

> Can a woman forget her nursing child, or show no compassion for the child of her womb? Even these may forget, yet I will not forget you. See, I have inscribed you on the palms of my hands (Is 49:15-16).

God demands total commitment not only from the chosen people in general but especially from each individual. Deuteronomy demands that parents drill this into their children:

> Hear, O Israel! The Lord our God is one Lord; and you shall love the Lord your God with all your heart, and with all your souls, and with all your might. And these words which I command you this day shall

be upon your heart; and you shall teach them diligently to your children, and shall talk of them when you sit in your house, and when you walk by the way, and when you lie down, and when you rise. And you shall bind them as a sign upon hand, fix them as an emblem on your forehead, and write them on the doorposts of your house and on your gates. (Dt 6: 4-9)

The New Covenant cemented in the sacrificial offering of the Lamb of God extends the marriage of God to man and man to God. Jesus teaches the identical commitment of each person to His Father, as He repeats Deuteronomy (Mk 12:29-30) and even seems to over-emphasize it: "Whoever comes to me and does not hate father and mother, wife and children and even life itself, cannot be my disciple" (Lk 14:26). This is the strongest statement of unity and exclusivity of God's love in Jesus Christ for each human person and the obvious need to respond.

Yet the very exclusiveness of love demanded from each human being for God, is precisely the identical exclusiveness totally predicated by the scriptures for wives and husbands for each other as they participate in that same unconditional mutual surrender between Christ and His Church (Eph 5:21-33).

Universal Vocation

This is also the meaning of the New Testament in which Christ becomes the bridegroom and all Christians the bride. It is within the context of covenant theology that children ought to learn their unique importance in the world. Each child is the result of a love affair between God and a special way of being reflected outside Himself which has never before and will never again exist in the world. That gift must be given back completely and in its entirety in body and soul in one of the three possible states in the world: virginity and celibacy given back to God directly in religious love service whether in religious order or priesthood, a single celibacy dedicated to God until such time or unless a suitable partner comes along, and finally, a gift in Christian matrimony that enables the individuals actually to experience in a deep personal way the personal love of Christ for His Church and of the Church for Christ. It is within this context that children are to be brought into being so that they can experience God's love for them through the unique and exclusive love of the parents for each other and for each child differently from every other child!

In the other scriptural stories there are many opportunities to present to children of every age level the various aspects of Christian chastity. In the Old Testament one can explain the entire area of Adam and Eve and their inhabiting of paradise followed by original sin with various examples applicable today. We can explain to children that clothing is valuable because it protects our integrity and intimacy. Just as they want their own toys and their own clothing so also they do not easily or ought not share their bodies with any others whether to view or touch. They should have it explained that their uneasiness when unclothed is quite good, natural and human. It is self-respect and self-regard. And further, they should understand that the invasion of another person's privacy of body is like reading another person's letter without the warrant to do so. Later, after sin, it can be explained to the children that, like Adam and Eve, once the human being makes up his own rules, he basically loses control of himself. (If I decide what food is good for me, I will soon be obese or malnourished!) So that when Adam and Eve decided to invent their own good and evil and to decide what was good for them to do or not, they found self-control difficult. Therefore they had to use clothing, not so much to protect their own privacy, but because of the temptation to invade the privacy of other body persons or to trigger such invasion by others.

Ten Commandments

The Ten Commandments should always be explained to children as the negative minimum that an individual must avoid in order to pursue the real goods of God, themselves and their neighbors. The commandment, "Love God above all things, and your neighbor as yourself" is repeated in the Ten Commandments in minimum negative fashion. The first three Commandments indicate that one is not to prefer any human goals or human pursuit of power to God Himself. God is the source of all aliveness and to prefer some aspect of my being alive to the source of aliveness is to cut myself off even from the good I pursue — like the astronaut who wants to do a space walk without his space suit or an "umbilical cord" tied to the space craft.

The other Ten Commandments, from 4 to 10, are concerned with human goods. Just as I ought not to cut myself off from God as my life source, so I ought not cut myself off from my life source on earth, my parents. I must love them, because without them, no matter what they have failed to do, I would not exist at all. In loving my neighbor, the least I can do is not betray him by attempting to make his spouse unfaithful to him. The least I can do in helping him to reach his fulfillment in knowledge is not lie to him or not steal those goods which enable him to be free and not a slave. The least I can do in helping him be fully alive is not kill him. And to prevent any of these things from happening, I ought not to develop such greed, envy, jealousy as will lead me sooner or later to seduce his wife, kill or harm him, betray him to his enemies, or take from him his means of livelihood.

Once the positive values protected by the Ten Commandments are taught to the children, they can be taught in negative fashion, in which case, of course, there must be clear definitions of adultery. In its simplest form adultery is the giving or receiving of the love which belongs between a husband and wife to someone who is not the committed partner. Since the value is total, mutual, exclusive self-gift, body and soul, to one person of the opposite sex for a lifetime with openness to children, any action against this is obviously a sin against the value of love-commitment in matrimony. This is clear from John Paul II's clear teaching on the nuptial meaning of the body. Obviously then, marital contraceptive sex (which is mutual use of partner as mere object), masturbation (often called self-abuse), fornication (usually referred to as pre-marital or pre-ceremonial sex), petting to orgasm (also called "heavy" petting, and which is the use of a partner for a mutual masturbatory release) and homosexuality in practice are nothing but conclusions from the principle "Thou shalt not commit adultery" (cf. H. Vernon Sattler, "Adultery within Marriage," *Homiletic and Pastoral Review,* Dec. 1981, pp. 24-47; and "Lust — Greatest of Sins?" *ibid.* Mar 1983, pp. 27-31).

In St. Matthew's Gospel (19:3-13) the teacher will find the entire teaching on marital love, fidelity and chastity, celibacy or virginity for God's kingdom, and the special place for children in Our Lord's teaching. The passage condemns divorce and re-marriage for either husband or wife, and does not permit justification for divorce even for the infidelity of the partner. The so-called exception clause ("except for unchastity" Mt 5:32 and 19:9) refers only to separation of man and woman who are wrongfully living in an invalid union (Cf. Commentary in *The Navarre Bible, Matthew* [Four Courts Press, Dublin] pp. 62-64 and 162-163). The passage on divorce is immediately followed by the teaching of Christ on

His special love for children and their special place in the kingdom of heaven (vv. 14-15).

The conclusion of this passage on those "who make themselves eunuchs for the sake of the kingdom of heaven," and the final: "Let anyone accept this who can" Mt 19:12) teach the basic *vocation* to chastity (cf. below) for all Christians (and indeed for all who are bound by the natural law). Absolute sexual abstinence is appropriate for those devoted absolutely to the kingdom of God in spreading the Good News. Temporary or periodic abstinence is expected by the vocational situation of not yet being married, or within marriage when such circumstances as separation, illness, prudent contraindications might render love union temporarily unwise. This includes the virtuous practice of *Natural Family Planning*, or, a better term, *Aware Parenting*. (Cf. John Paul II, *On the Family*, ¶¶ 32-33.)

Virtue System

Children should be taught about the virtues.

A virtue is a habit of mind or will which makes it easy to know and will the truths and decisions necessary for human flourishing in God's plan for men. Faith, hope and charity are the supernatural Christian virtues, which are infused with the grace of conversion and/or baptism. Prudence, justice, fortitude and temperance are the natural cardinal virtues (on which all the other virtues swing as upon so many hinges) of the will. They are to be supernaturalized in Christian living by the grace of God obtained through the sacraments and prayer.

The Supernatural Virtues

All the supernatural virtues are the direct gifts of God in the Holy Spirit and cannot be acquired or intensified by one's own efforts. Nor can we successfully pray for any one of them. On the contrary, prayer itself already implies the pre-existence of the supernatural virtues. This is why as we begin the rosary, we usually begin by a Pater and three Aves for "an *increase* of the virtues of faith, hope and charity." We ought to pray constantly for such a deeper infusion of these virtues.

Faith

Faith is the virtue granted by God which enables the human person to assent to God revealing and to the content of His revelation. It includes the acceptance of the word of God, whether as His Son revealing Himself to us, or as revealed through sacred scripture and sacred tradition. It also asks us to assent to truths which may be written out in propositions or statements derived from what God has revealed to us, and taught infallibly by the Church whether by *de fide* definitions (formal definitions by Councils or by the Pope in *ex cathedra* teaching), or by the universal and ordinary magisterial authority of the Church. Finally, Christian Faith demands that we give *religious assent* of mind and will to the ordinary teaching of the church in doctrinal and moral matters —not necessarily to policy decisions, though filial obedience to these should be anticipated. (Cf. Vatican II, *Lumen Gentium* ¶ 25, and *Dei Verbum,* ¶10.)

Religious assent of mind and will is something like, though far superior to, the medical faith I have in my physician. I believe him because I *trust* his medical knowledge. I believe *what* he tells me about my diabetes and *obey* his prescriptions (his orders!). I know nothing about medicine or my illnesses. I trust him even though I do not understand and might be most unhappy about his commands. If I refuse him medical assent, I equivalently reject his teaching and look for another doctor. For his part he rightly refuses to treat me for anything if I distrust him in a single diagnosis. If I have no knowledge and go to him for the truth and direction, I have no reason to select from what he teaches me. If I lose faith in him in one thing, I lose faith in all. There is no such thing as "pick and choose" faith.

Faith is very important in the area of sex education (or to repeat — chastity education). It is faith which teaches each individual his own unique inviolability, his value as a special creative act of God and his worth as purchased by the very Body and Blood in redemption. Only faith will enable a child to see that Christian matrimony is the union of one man to one woman in the name of and in place of Jesus Christ and His Church. Only faith will enable the acceptance of the indissolubility of marriage in an apparently impossible union involving mental or physical illness and possible serious immorality. Only faith will enable a person to see in what seems to be an apparently boring, repetitious and pedestrian family life the will of God and the achievement of His purposes. Only faith will see that a Christian must bring a chaste nuptial gift of body to the marriage bed, and that all sexual sins (no need to enumerate them) will destroy marital joys, goods, values, whether outside or within marriage. Apologetic (explanatory) natural law reasoning will reinforce and bring insight into faith here, but reason will never overcome a will not to believe.

Hope

Hope is the virtue which trusts that God will provide the graces to enable the individual to live up to his vocation to be a Christian, and to be a servant of God as a Christian, in celibacy or matrimony. It is the virtue particularly necessary to overcome human failings and arbitrary sinfulness. A person without hope cannot avoid the despair of ever being forgiven by God, spouse, neighbor, parents or children! Without hope, the person will neither strive for vocational fulfillment or to reach even the level of confessing his sins in repentance. Only hope will prevent suicide, whether such an attitude is actually carried out (the extinction of life) or only attempted by escape through drug, alcohol, or sexual addictions; neurotic hysteria, compulsivities or even absolute self-despisement. Only hope can look in the mirror and say "You're a poor thing, baby, but you're the only me I've got in Christ." Or better, "Be patient with me, *God* is not finished with me yet." Best: "Smile! God still loves you as you are, but too much to leave you that way!"

Charity

The idea of Christian charity is much deeper than a generic kind of love, or general benevolence which seems to be a humanistic concept. And it is certainly much more than the giving which we call almsgiving. It is not merely affection, or desire for what is missing. Charity, for the Christian, is a love (*ágape* in Greek) which only God can express and which He enables men to express *in His place* by sanctifying grace. It is a love which is *creative* of the goodness which it loves into being. It is the love which Jesus exerts through us which makes the apparently unlovable to be lovable, to redeem what seems beyond redemption, to forgive one who is even rejective of forgiveness, and in the forgiving make that person worthy of the forgiveness through the gift of sorrow (tears!). It is not that we have loved God, but that He has first loved us, and we are called to love others before they come to love us (cf. I John).

Though divine charity is necessary for every Christian and for every kind of human relationship, it is especially necessary for any nuptial commitment of woman to man and man to woman, and between parents and their children. No human being is quite worth loving with the kind of total self-gift which is demanded of Christian matrimony and celibacy. Only Christ can give your husband or wife or child the kind of love he or she needs to become what the creative act of God has designed, and to overcome failures and refusals to achieve that end. This is why the decision of Christ to love His Church and to demand a certain kind of love from her is described in the love of man for woman and woman for man (Eph 5: 21-33). It is only in such a mutual devotion in divine charity that the mutual but real inferiorities and superiorities of marriage and family life become utterly irrelevant. Christian marital love is not a 50-50 proposition.

Children may on occasion be cute and draw some kind of sentimental affection but they are not very lovable in themselves. They become what they ought to be only by being loved into existence again and again. Nor in their endless, bottomless, emptiness of receptivity (Gimme!) are they able to respond adequately to the love of their parents. Again, only a love which is creative and redemptive in Jesus Christ by the parents will eventually evoke from the children the kind of maturity which will be a reasonable facsimile of a Christian human being! Children learn not only that "home is the place where, when you go there, they have to take you in!" but also that they themselves are the home members who love the family members because they need to be loved, not only because or when they are nice.

It is the un-self-consciousness of this necessary love which makes the children cry when their parents are in conflict, and which is devastating to them when a father or mother divorces or separates or expresses hatred for the other parent. The matrix into which psychological personhood is poured is the unquestionable, creative, redemptive, forgiving love of parents. John Paul II teaches that "man is the only creature that God loves for himself (the human's self! not God's self)" God does not *possess*, He *frees* whom He loves for utter fulfillment. This is particularly the goal of nuptial and family love — to express this Divine Love in Christ-Church.

This must be repeatedly taught in religious education, with special reference to the scriptural passages of love, the crucified love of Christ, the necessity of loving *first*, forgiving till "seventy times seven" etc. (For more on the natural and supernatural kinds of love, especially as expressed in the paradigm of marital love, see H. Vernon Sattler, *All About Love*, University of Scranton, Scranton PA, 1985).

Prayer

Though the virtues of faith, hope and charity must precede prayer, prayer is important to beg God to increase these three virtues. The most important aspect of this prayer, however, is not so much the prayer of petition, but the prayer of contemplation which dwells with the light and ever growing insight upon the interpersonal communication of being between Father and Son and their mutual Spiration of the Holy Spirit in the Holy Trinity, and the communication on the matrimonial and life-giving level between Christ and His Church. This is meditation and all Christians need it in the way that they need to become aware of their own personhood.

The Cardinal Virtues

There are four fundamental moral virtues upon which all the others *hinge*. This is the meaning of the word cardinal! The cardinal virtues, however, presuppose the choice of true human fulfillment on the road to God as good. If I do not intensely choose God above all things, and my neighbor as myself, and also choose for him what is truly fulfilling of him or her — liberty, knowledge, creativity, fulfillment of bodily abilities, real creative playfulness — I will not practice any of the cardinal virtues well.

Prudence

Prudence is the habitual choice of means of legitimately chosen and pursued goals. If I know that I ought to love God above all things, I will prudentially choose times to read the scriptures and to pray meditatively. If I want to love my wife, I will choose very carefully the present for our anniversary or her birthday and keep her constantly in my mind and my imagination, lest I become a lazy lover, become bored and take her for granted. If I want to understand the nature of marriage, and of love, the differences between the sexes and how to control appetites, I will choose very wisely the kind of reading I ought to do, the companions I choose, the conversations I engage in, etc., etc.

A similar type of activity, yet the very opposite of prudence, is used when I choose apt means to evil goals. A murderer or thief will plot every step of his procedure to accomplish his goals and he will look almost as identically careful as a prudent man in the pursuit of true love, but we call his choices craftiness or deceit.

Justice

Justice is the virtue which disposes an individual to give to another his or her due. It is the minimum for the first part of the golden rule: "Love your neighbor as you love yourself." The least I can do for my neighbor is not take from him whatever he owns or is his right. Justice is very, very important in family life. Very early children complain that parents are not fair, or even play favorites, to an extraordinary degree. Husbands and wives have entered into a covenant of matrimony. But a covenant though it is *more* than a contract is nevertheless still a contract. Adultery, for example, is an injustice to the spouse as well as a violation of chastity. The two have committed themselves to each other in a contract to give and receive mutual services on every bodily, emotional, intellectual and spiritual level. The marriage covenant as already explained is more binding than a contract, not less binding.

Fortitude

Fortitude is courage, the habitual ability to continue the pursuit of a goal against all obstacles and to repeatedly work toward such goals after apparent failures. It is the intestinal strength to keep beating one's head against the wall when the whole process seems senseless and futile. Fortitude is necessary for a young person, boy or girl, to reach maturity, to continue to struggle for the integration of all one's personal abilities into a single unique personality. Especially important is fortitude in the overcoming of temptations against chastity and modesty.

Today it is extremely difficult not only to admit but even to be proud of one's sexual integrity as still virginal and not to join the gang in boasting of a sexual prowess they probably do not at all have. It takes very great courage for a young woman not to rival all her companions in their pursuit of sexiness and immodesty of dress. Socially it is always easier to "Go with the flow." It takes fortitude of fantastic proportions for a young man to overcome the adolescent passions which lead (more than 99% of boys) into lengthy bouts with masturbation on their way to maturity. The absence of young men from the confessional at the present time is a very clear sign that most have given up the struggle or have convinced themselves that nothing is wrong with the masturbatory approach. Yet nothing will destroy their marriages more completely than an approach to their girlfriends and wives with the playboy or masturbatory attitude. These attitudes reduce a woman to a mere thing, puppet, doll, service-station — de-personalizing her even when she is unaware of it. Every woman, even when she is desirous of admiring looks, feels her skin crawl when subjected to clearly lustful eyes.

Temperance

The virtue which controls and *directs* all the fundamental human impulses is called temperance. Unfortunately, the impression is given that temperance is opposed to passion, enthusiasm or intensity of emotion. The impression cannot be otherwise because, since original sin, the human passions tend to be more turbulent than lacking in intensity. They seem to be needing more control by repression than control by direction. It is important to see that the direction of passionate impulse is equally important to the control of its erratic release. The baseball pitcher with the most powerful fast ball is soon relegated to the minor leagues if he cannot control it to put it over the plate.

Temperance is not pale and passionless. Algernon Swinburne is in error when he cries blasphemously, "Thou hast conquered, oh pale Galilean, the world has grown grey from thy breath." Though Spring is the most temperate of seasons, it is also the most passionate, "June is *bustin" out* all over!"

Though St. Thomas Aquinas, in his treatise on temperance, spends most of his time on the control of the various human appetites by way of discipline of them, he initiates his study by pointing out that, though one vice against this cardinal virtue is intemperance, the opposite vice would be insensibility. The person who has no appetite for food and needs to force himself to eat is no less ill than the person who cannot stop eating in his compulsivity towards obesity. Anorexia nervosa (distaste for food) and bulimia (gorging) are really just two manifestations of the same disorder of appetite. It is the same compulsive fascination with eating that leads to loss of appetite or compulsive fixation upon food.

The virtues within the cardinal virtue of temperance which focus upon sexual activity are chastity, modesty and continence.

Chastity

Chastity is the virtue which controls and directs the sexual appetites towards their goals, which are the expression of total self-gift of one man to one woman and vice versa for a life time and with unity, exclusivity and openness to procreative potential. As indicated in another section of this book (Chapter 2), the meaning of sexual intercourse is a triumphant celebration of two-in-one-flesh. It is celebrated with most intensity and with most passion when two virginal people enter Christian matrimony and discover their own unique and incommunicable language of mutual penetration in love.

Chastity is called *perfect chastity* when it promises virginity in total openness to the day by day inspiration of the Holy Spirit in religious service whether in clergy or cloister. It is called chastity or virginity in the world if it attempts to maintain self-integrity unless and until God sends a spouse, a beloved, to invite the other into a Christian marriage. This is called virginity in the world, if embraced for life, or pre-marital chastity until marriage.

But Christian marriage celebrated as a commitment to a state in which "no one has gone this way before and no one but you will ever go this way again" is called *chaste wedlock*. It is revealing and should be most inspiring to married couples to recall that Pius XI in 1930 wrote his masterful encyclical on Christian marriage and entitled it with its first two words, *Casti Connubii — On Chaste Wedlock*. Chastity is not coldness, frigidity, impotence, distaste, rejection. It is passionate focus and expression towards one's only beloved: God or the one called by Him to take His place in giving and receiving love in Christ.

Purity

It is customary among Catholics to talk about chastity and purity as the same identical virtue. But really purity is a broader concept than chastity. Purity means singleness, unmixed, unadulterated. A candle of pure beeswax contains no admixture of tallow, or oil, or anything else. Purity in the spiritual sense means the love of God above all without any selfishness. St. Augustine defined purity in perfection as "Amor Dei usque ad contemptum sui" ("Love of God unto even the contempt of self"), and absolute evil or sin as "amor sui usque ad contemptum Dei"

("Love of self to the very contempt of God!") In sexual matters purity means the absence of lust and acceptance of love-union as the total gift of self to the beloved in marriage, without any self-conditions. Our Pope John Paul II defines spousal love as the total gift of self to the other.

Lust

Many people misunderstand the nature of lust. Lust does not refer to mere bodily sexual passion, which is intensely good as the accompaniment of total mutual surrender. Lust is the focus upon bodily satisfaction for oneself exclusive of all other meaning. It is the sexual passion referred to by every woman who complains of being merely used, treated as a thing or sexual service-station, who rejects pornography as sexual abuse, and which makes her resent the ogling of other women by her husband, or his penchant for erotic reading or pictures. On the other hand, it is what the immodestly seductive woman wants to trigger in a man.

Continence

Continence is merely the strong **"No!"** which is necessary to control a sudden and apparently uncontrollable sexual passion. It takes no time to reason or argue. It acts.

Modesty

Modesty is the virtue which controls access to the passion of sexual *love*. Scripture clearly indicated this in insisting for the bride: "A garden locked is my sister, my bride, a garden locked, a fountain sealed" (Song of Songs 4:12); and for the groom: "Do not stir up or awaken love until it is ready!" (8:4)

The virtue of modesty has slightly different emphases in application to the problems of boys and girls. A young woman correctly wishes to be attractive precisely as a woman and therefore she wishes to be happy with her sexual charms and beauty, and rightly so. She wishes to be loved and therefore cuddled, hugged, petted, touched. Finally, she wishes to surrender herself to someone who will sweep her off her feet in passionate interpenetration. All of these things she will achieve hopefully and completely in marriage. Her problem is how to be reasonably attractive, without invoking from the onlooker, by-stander or companion, the kind of sexual access which is reserved only for marriage spouses, or the lust for such.

For adolescents, it might be important to indicate that the celebration of love union is the positive use of the very wooing rituals which would be sinful outside the marital surrender, lest they somehow think that intimacies are at least suspect even in marriage.

On his side, a boy wishes to look, see, touch, explore, and ultimately to conquer and pour himself out into his beloved. No amount of sexual curiosity will ever satisfy him because, with Don Juan, he is tempted to believe that he will be a great "lover" if he samples the maximum number of bodies. He will never fully comprehend that the fullness of experience is by lending himself to that one person, and not by possessing many in passing superficial encounters, (cf. Thomas Howard, *Chance or the Dance* [Ignatius Press] 139-142).

Moral Principles For Chastity

All true and real goods are protected by laws or rules which govern them. Good health demands: "Thou shalt not smoke!" among many other rules. Innocent human life demands that it remain inviolable to all direct attacks: "Do no murder!" But sin is the heart and not only in the action. To will the death of an enemy or even to approvingly day-dream of feeding him as bait to a piranha, is the same violation of the Fifth Commandment as murdering him in fact. So also, suicide in self-hatred or despair.

Love union and the intense sexual passion which accompanies it is reserved in its significance and consequences to matrimony (cf. Chapter II above, and below on the sacrament of matrimony). It is so valuable there that it is a serious sin elsewhere. Good sexual love-making is protected by: "Thou shalt not commit adultery" and "Thou shalt not covet thy neighbor's wife!" These are generic commandments which found chastity (cf. above on chastity).

Venereal or sexual pleasure is that pleasure which is experienced when the genital organs are strongly aroused (erection in the male, tumescence [swelling] and lubrication of the genital region and breasts in the female), and completed in very pleasurable paroxysms called orgasm, with the ejection of semen into the body of the woman. This pleasure arises before, during and is still in action in the act of mutual sexual surrender. It is so good in marriage that its value is protected by negatives of the sixth commandment. Therefore, to deliberately bring about even the slightest venereal pleasure without relation to married love-making, or to will it or day-dream about it with wilful approval is a serious sin. This is the evil not only of fornication and adultery, but also of masturbation and "lust in the heart" (cf. Mt 5:28), as well as marital contracepting and mere (even mutually agreed) lust.

Moral Principles For Modesty

Reverence for the goodness of innocent human life demands not only the avoidance of murder, suicide, hatred, but also a consideration of signs of respect for the privacy, and courtesies surrounding the sacredness of person. Similarly, modesty is the virtue which approaches sexual love-making with awe, respect, and surrounds it with privacy, ritual, clothing, hesitance, etc. Granting that one is unwilling to consent to sexual pleasure in thought, desire or deed outside a committed marital surrender, modesty demands that one ought not risk sexual arousal through imagination, reading, touch, undress, viewing, etc., without a reason proportionate to the risk of *undesired* arousal. Obviously, such activity engaged *in order to* arouse sexual passion inappropriately is already a serious sin. The area of curiosity, reasonable sexual knowledge during early adolescence, reasonable sexual knowledge in view of preparation for marriage, reasonable swim wear, or recognition of virile or feminine attractiveness, have different and sliding scale norms depending on the individuals involved. This is one of the reasons for even secular concern with the viewing audience of motion pictures (G, PG, PG-13, R, NC-17, and X). Catholic audiences grade much more severely, since our secular world demands a sexual revolution in which venereal pleasure is never wrong alone or between consenting adults of any gender, and seems undesirable only when forced (rape) or imposed by relatives (incest).

Catholic norms for viewing of the probably arousing are much more severe (A for general audiences, and A-II, A-III, A-IV for older children, adolescents, adults only, and O, objectionable, at least in part, for all!). Unfortunately, a mere visit to the local cinema would prove that not even the secular norms are being followed in practice! Parochial schools and schools of religion should teach that these guidelines are moral norms for all, and especially for the practice and the discipline of children. Children should be taught that parents have serious obligations in conscience to guide film and TV viewing, and that they must respect this obligation and obey their parents.

Fertility Awareness

From the earliest simple information of sexual meaning, it should be made clear to the child that the procreation of a human person is quite different from the reproduction by animals. The human person ought to come into being only from the unreserved personal and bodily self-surrender of husband and wife to each other. Whenever there is school teaching on biological reproduction, no matter how simple in early years, or more complete in later adolescence, a boy should always be made aware that semen is the source of his husbanding a wife and his fathering of a child. The young woman should always be aware that ovulation produces the ovum which will possibly make her a mother. It is much more important to teach the adolescent girl about ovulation than about menstruation. John Paul II insists that every Catholic couple today should be instructed in their mutual fertility awareness, and the significance of loving respect for their mutual fertility (*Familiaris Consortio* ¶ 32-35, 66). This is often called Natural Family Planning, but would be better dubbed *Fertility Awareness*. "Planning" in our modern speech seems to mean arbitrary pre-programming of a pre-determined result. This is the meaning of *Planned Parenthood* which really means programmed non-parenthood on the one hand, and only pre-programmed parenthood on the other (even by artificial insemination or *in vitro* fertilization). For the Christian, planning means the decision to act prudently and accept the inherent results of the action. Contraceptionists insist: "Children by (antecedently planned) choice, not by chance." Christians know that the advent of a child and every happy or unhappy experience of him is always a chance, a surprise! One plans to eat dinner and accept the nutritional results. If one tends to obesity, he cuts down his intake and avoids pleasurable snacks, he does not depend on liposuction or induced vomiting or cathartics (bulimia). The artist does not program his masterpiece, he paints and is happily surprised if the result is great.

The Sacraments

The nature of a sacrament in general is a material or bodily sign of a deeply important reality which tends to or actually makes that reality to be present. For example the natural sacrament of sexual intercourse not only signs interpersonal communion among husband and wife and child. It also makes that communion real (Cf. Chapter II on the meaning of sexual intercourse). Such a sacrament is also inviolable. The sacrament of speech demands the inviolability of words as truthful. A lie is a "sacrilege" of speech. Contraception is a violation of the sacrament of love-union.

On the supernatural level, a sacrament is a materially significant act which really makes a supernatural reality to be present. The fundamental supernatural sacrament is the human nature of Christ as the covenantal (nuptial!) sacrament of God. The divine and human natures are wedded in the bodily existence of Jesus Christ. The Church is the covenantal (nuptial!) sacrament of Jesus Christ. It is very important to see that though St. Paul is teaching mutual deference of husband and wife to each other in Ephesians 5, the ultimate analogue is the marital and fecund unity of Christ and the Church into which each Christian is born through the "womb" of baptism. The mystery is the unity of Christ-Church into which baptized husband and wife will enter when they receive the sacrament of matrimony (read Ephesians 5: 21-33). Try to recall that the Mystical Body analogy of Christ as Head and Church as Body is not the image of the human body in which the head is just a part of the body. It is a marital or covenantal unity of Christ as Spouse and the Church as Espoused. The image is of husband as head, and wife as "other self."

The Sacramental System

The Church has solemnly defined that there are seven sacraments in the ritual activity of the Church, seven action-signs which make Christ present under different aspects of presence. Usually these are listed in the order in which they are received, a logical or temporal order: baptism, confirmation, penance, holy eucharist, sacrament of the sick, and then two sacraments of vocation are listed, matrimony and holy orders. It seems to this author that these sacraments ought to exist in a psychological, and more basically, an ontological order (the order of existential importance). At least, it might be helpful for a teacher to experience their value in the following order: eucharist, matrimony, orders, baptism, confirmation, penance and sacrament of the sick. They are presented here with emphasis on their importance to chastity and modesty.

Eucharist

The eucharist (the Holy Sacrifice of the Mass with a continuation of the divine presence of Jesus under the sacramental species of bread and wine) is **the** sacrament above all others. It is the divine wedding feast of divine-human marriage in Christ extended to the end of time. Jesus Christ is present here as priest, victim, and sustenance. He is the sacrificial lamb of the New Covenant (cf. above for covenantal theology) which He Himself makes present on the altar through the priest who acts *in persona Christi Capitis* (in the bodily person of Christ the Head [Spouse!]) in saying: "This is **My** Body! This is **My** Blood!" This spousal body-presence is offered as sustenance to all the baptized as a holy communion (being-one-with) with Him in the flesh and with all other baptized in the flesh (significance of the kiss of peace).

Obviously, respect for the sacredness of one's own body, the bodies of all others of either sex, the bodies of children, within or outside marriage is founded upon the eucharistic food of the body of Christ, which is offered to every baptized person and ultimately to all called to become Christians. Whatever we do to other human beings in deed, word or thought is done to Christ Himself. "Because you have done it to one of these my least brethren, you did it to me" (cf. Mt 25:31-46).

Christian chastity and modesty is founded upon eucharistic awe both outside of and within matrimony. The priest who sins mortally in a sexual manner in thought, word or deed, must not say Mass, distribute holy communion (or absolve penitents, cf. below) without first approaching the sacrament of penance, or in emergency, crying from his heart as perfect an act of contrition as he can, with determination to approach the power of the keys in the confessional as soon as possible. The same thing is true of permanent deacons, lay ministers of holy communion, and any persons who receive any of the so-called sacraments of the living (confirmation, holy communion, matrimony, orders, or even the sacrament of the sick [unless unconscious]). Those conscious of the guilt of deliberate lust, masturbation, extra-marital "petting," fornication, adultery, sodomy, active homosexual practices, marital contraception, serious immodesty which deliberately enters the occasions of sexual sin must not approach the holy table without penance!

Unfortunately, it has become so universal for everyone to approach and receive the eucharist that little thought is given to this requirement.

Even strangers who do not know what they are doing often come up to receive. But St. Paul warns: "Whoever, therefore, eats the bread or drinks the cup of the Lord in an unworthy manner will be answerable for the body and blood of the Lord. Examine yourself and only then eat of the bread and drink of the cup. For all who eat and drink without discerning the body eat and drink judgment against themselves" (I Cor 11:27-29).

Children old enough to understand must be taught not to ask their peers or elders why they might not be receiving holy communion at Mass. Parents ought not probe their children's (or each other's) consciences either.

In seminaries and convents, in days gone by, penance was regularly made available before Mass, and often, in parish churches confessions were heard before every Mass. It is unbelievable that in the blatant appeal to libidinous eros in the media which floods our senses, that there could be fewer failures in chastity and modesty demanding repentance!

This awe and fear of the possibility of desecrating the bodily presence of Jesus Christ in the eucharist is a powerful motive for chastity and modesty for all young people. Holy communion has often been called the bread of angels in this regard. But this idea is dangerous. It allows some to think that we are but pure spirits imprisoned in a recalcitrant body (a misinterpretation of St. Paul when he complains and longs to be delivered from the "body of this death" Rom 7:24). Holy communion provides contact with the *body* not merely the spirit of Christ. It makes me love and never merely use or abuse my own body as a participant in His body.

It is a tradition of Catholic education that frequent attendance at the eucharist with reception of Christ's body and blood is necessary for the purities of chastity and modesty. The desire to receive the eucharist provides motives for sexual purity. The reception of the eucharist worthily provides the graces to achieve, and re-achieve once lost, the virtue of chastity and its hedge, modesty.

Matrimony

As the eucharist is the invitation to the whole world to ultimately enter into a holy communion with God and with each other, and is thus an universal offering of God-Man to *all*, matrimony is the sacrament of the God-Man's offer of life-giving union with each person *exclusively*, and the invitation to the spouses to enter into that exclusive, total and mutual self-surrender of Christ to the Church and the Church to Christ. Matrimony is the sacrament of sexuality (cf. Sattler, "The Sacrament of Sexuality," *Communio*, Winter 1981; reprinted in *Social Justice Review*, Dec. 1986; Jan.-Feb. 1987; also Sattler, *Sex Is Alive and Well and Flourishing Among Christians*, passim). Simply, when St. Paul is inveighing against impurity, he speaks of this sacred love union: "Do you know that your bodies are members of Christ? ... you were bought with a price, so glorify God in your body" (I Cor 6:13-20). It is the unbelievable sacredness of the sacramental surrender of marital sexuality which precludes all sins of self-centered lust, unchastity and sinful immodesty. Marriage is not a license for lust. Marital love-union is the reason that lust (sexual passion for selfish release) is evil.

Teachers, of course, must be models of nuptial love for their students, whether they are virginal persons (priest, nuns, lay) or married. If for any reason the "life-style" of the teacher is not imitable, the minimum a teacher can do would be to insist that the children know what the real truth is, and that not every example should be followed! Teachers publicly known to be living a sexual life-style that defies clear magisterial teaching on the sanctity of sex as reserved to the total significance of Christian matrimony or celibacy should not teach or model Catholic doctrine under Catholic auspices. At the very least, as must a leering father, a teacher must suggest: "Don't do as I do, do as I say." This is not hypocritical if the teacher truly believes what he says!

In the Catholic school or school of religious education attendance at a wedding Mass, the analysis of the wedding ritual, discussion of the variously apt scriptural passages suggested in the Roman Ritual, a project of planning a truly Catholic wedding ceremony, discussion of liturgically proper music, as well as the explanation of the significance of canonical impediments, requirements of the Church concerned with the proper preparation for marriage and the Church's anxious concern about mixed or ecumenical marriages will all provide formation on chaste wedlock, as well as pre-wedlock chastity, and even the significance of celibacy-virginity.

Orders

As the eucharist is the sign of the universal love of God in Christ for all mankind, and matrimony is the sign of the exclusive love of God in

Christ for each and every individual (Christ-Church love of spouses open to God's creativity of a child), the sacrament of orders is the making of Christ present again in a priest, enabling him to act *in persona Christi capitis*. To this very day, only Christ can be our priest, king and teacher. He did not cease to be with His Church at His ascension. He is sacramentally present in the bishop and the priest who makes the bishop present in each parish. Only a priest who embodies Jesus Christ sacramentally can *effectively* say: "This is *my* body! *I* absolve you from your sins!" and make these realities happen. Anyone, or even a puppet, can say the words as merely functional noises. Only the ordained male can make Christ sacramentally present as sacrificer, absolver, authoritative teacher, ruler. Others may share and provide helpful assistance, but "the buck stops here."

Celibacy is obviously appropriate for orders, which involves a nuptial devotion to the Church and each individual among the People of God. Christ says so as He extols "eunuchs for the Kingdom of Heaven" (Mt 19:12). John Paul II insists that the People of God have the right to observe the priest's fidelity to celibacy as a norm of their own nuptial fidelity!

Confirmation

The sacrament of confirmation is the sacrament which makes one mature in Christ. It is a kind of sacrament of adolescence reaching supernatural adulthood. St. Paul urges his converts to strive in the Holy Spirit: '. . . until all of us come to the unity of the faith and of the knowledge of the Son of God, to maturity, to the measure of the full stature of Christ" (Eph 4:13). It is similar to the Bar-Mitzva for a Jewish boy after which the adolescent is expected to fully observe all of the Jewish Torah, from which till that point he was largely exempt as too immature to live its rigors! Though confirmation is often conferred early in life, today it is usually delayed to the beginning of puberty. Confirmation is the sacrament of the challenge of Christian adulthood. At all events it is wise to use the occasion of the reception of confirmation to urge the maturity of Christ which demands the striving and grace necessary for the self-control and direction of all the disturbing drives of adolescence: the natural desire for gradual independence from authority, the day-dreaming of romantic and adventuresome achievements, the psychological effects of masculine (testosterone) or feminine (estrogen, progesterone) hormones, the temptations and curiosities toward sexual prowess and seductivity, the calls of Christian vocationalism. The gifts of the Holy Spirit, and the fruits of the Holy Spirit should be explained at the time of confirmation, not only in themselves but in their application to chastity and modesty.

Penance

The sacrament of penance, now called the sacrament of reconciliation, is the sacrament instituted by Christ in which conscious personal sin is submitted to a priest who acts *in persona Christi capitis* (in the very person of Christ the Head) for judgment, imposes penalty (satisfactory penance) and absolution if the penitent is properly disposed. In an earlier formula, after questioning, judging, teaching correct moral values, correcting erroneous conscience, and imposing penitential prayer or actions, the priest with designated power of the keys of the Kingdom from the bishop (called "faculties") said: "And I, by His very authority, absolve you from your sins in the name of the Father and of the Son and of the Holy Spirit." The new formula is less explicit, but the priest still says: *I absolve* you. . . etc."

Original Sin

Adam and Eve, by their arrogant sin of deciding to "know good and evil" (i.e. an absolute pro-choice position), lost their original innocence, and all the gifts which went with it, as well as the transition from earthly human life to heavenly life without experiencing what we now know as death. We were to inherit the original supernatural gift, but when they lost their treasure by sin, there was no such treasure to hand on to us as begotten heirs. The practical result of this is a downward tendency in every human being. We are given multiple human appetites for our integral fulfillment and flourishing as truly human, but since the fall of Adam and Eve, each of these appetites tends to pursue its own immediate satisfaction without reference to the total good and integrity of our person. G. K. Chesterton suggests that the effect is as of a man "who ran out of his house, jumped on his horse, and rode off in all directions at once." Anger is an emotion given to us to support our search for justice; since original sin it tends often to vicious vengeance. Sexual ecstasy is ours for total mutual unconditional surrender; after original sin it most often ends in selfish lust. St. Paul describes the effects of our inheritance of original sin:

> So I find it to be a law that when I want to do right, evil lies close at hand. For I delight in the law of God, in my inmost self, but I see in my members another law at war with the law of my mind and making me captive to the law of sin which dwells in my members. Wretched man that I am! Who will rescue me from this body of death? Thanks be to God through Jesus Christ Our Lord! (Rm 7:21-25)

Baptism removes the reality of the original sin of Adam and Eve but leaves the practical results of it still present with us, which can be analyzed under the rubric of the three concupiscences, and the seven capital sins.

The Concupiscences

The word concupiscence means the quick almost spontaneous arising of desire, and really is present in all our appetites. Unfortunately, most Catholics think of concupiscence only in considering the problem of sexual arousal, the spontaneous triggering of lust. But there are many concupiscences, so many that they are classified traditionally into three groups: the concupiscence of the flesh, the concupiscence of the eyes, and the pride of life (cf. 1 Jn 2:15). Though all three are with us all the time, each one has some impact upon the practice of chastity and modesty.

The teaching on the concupiscence of the flesh does not mean that the body has evil implanted in it. Roughly, it corresponds to what Freud called libido. At first, he thought this was purely sexual energy which could somehow be channeled (sublimated) into other areas. Before his death he saw libido as a generic drive from within which was expended in every vital function, among which sexual drive was just one. Generally, the concupiscences of the flesh are all those human drives which originate within the person, rather than from without. Hunger, thirst, muscular stimuli, dance, bodily playfulness, desire to listen, look, touch, run, jump, grasp, stretch, chew, feel comfort, pleasure, and much more — are all aspects of libido, or this concupiscence of the flesh. These drives are not evil in themselves, but they tend to abuse. Hunger can lead to "pigging out"; drink can trigger intoxication; pleasure can urge the use of euphoric drugs; sexual drive can incline to masturbation, seduction, fornication.

These various drives are connected with each other so that loss of control in one tends to spread to loss of control in the others. The drunken lecher is a classic literary caricature (e.g. in *Paint Your Wagon,* and Dolittle in *My Fair Lady*). The problem for growing children of both sexes is to show them how to harness and direct their very strong appetites towards true values. That specific aspect of libido which is sexual arousal is best referred to in connection with understanding all the "down under" appetites.

While the essence of the concupiscence of the flesh is being driven by appetites, the essence of the concupiscence of the eyes is drawn from the outside. Being drawn is roughly equivalent to the ancient idea of *eros,* the thrilling discovery that there is a great world out there of adventuresome experiences or romantic discoveries. Sometimes people think that libido and eros are identical. Freud first referred to libido as sexual arousal. Later he used eros to refer both to such arousal and sexual romance! It is true that one can eroticize libido, that is, one can romantically explore all sorts of libidinous experimentations with multiple partners, orifices, scenarios. But there are many other erotic experiences which need not involve libidinous activities at all! Falling in love is one of many erotic experiences. Eros can be the thrilling discovery that someone else is more important to my loving than I am to myself! It is a truly erotic experience to love a buddy, a teacher, a coach, a future spouse, a team-mate, a child, a spiritual director, Jesus Christ, God! Scripture describes it in terms of marital love which is applied among Jewish and Christian commentators to the love of man for God: "Draw me after you! Let us make haste. The king has brought me into his chambers. We will exult and rejoice in you, we will extol your love more than wine. . . " (Song of Songs 1:4-5).

The concupiscence of the eyes is best understood by reading Rollo May (*Love and Will,* esp. his two chapters on the daimonic). Positively, this "being drawn" leads to romantic and true love and creativity (e.g. in music, art, drama, making a home, evangelical zeal for the Gospel!). Negatively, this "being drawn" can be *de*monic, evil, destructive of goodness, and expressed in cruelty, torture, seductivity, even rape.

Though adolescents of both sexes must face both of these concupiscences, the first (of the flesh) seems to be more the experience of boys (since their testosterone makes them aggressive, driven) and the second is more the experience of girls (whose experience of estrogen which triggers ovulation and progesterone, which forwards bodily nesting of a possible baby, urges them to romantic nurturing).

The concupiscence of the pride of life is the quite natural appetite of the growing human being for independence from others, individual assertiveness, decisions which are truly their own. It is the same appetite the serpent triggered in Adam and Eve to invent their own personal and individual moral law! It is celebrated in Sammy Davis Jr.'s "I've Got to Be Me" and Sinatra's "I Did It My Way." It is the psychic trigger which occasions the crisis in Christian faith in almost every teenager. It starts with the early child's "why?" and ends with the insistence that one is "pro-choice" and therefore can make up one's own moral rights and wrongs with arrogant arbitrariness. Yet questioning is necessary if the adolescent is ever to be not only morally free but morally responsible! The problem is the change the defiant closed-minded "Show Me!" to a truly responsible but humble willingness to be overcome by objective truth.

The Capital Sins

In the negative sense, the three concupiscences can be analyzed in the so-called seven capital sins or the seven deadly sins: pride, covetousness, lust, anger, gluttony, envy and sloth. These are not independent of each other, and are not to be confused with the sins one falls into most often. They are rather the hidden motivations which underlie most of an individual's human acts of "cussedness." To discover which one of these is at the base of one's motivations is to discover one's "predominant fault." Often lust is considered the predominant drive of apparently randy adolescent boys. But a sin of unchastity might be triggered by covetousness of another's wife or girl-friend! Envy of the experiences boasted about in the locker room (which are often pure fantasy) may lead a girl or boy into seductive immodesty. Arrogant pride in spouses suggests that they can arbitrarily form their own consciences regarding marital contraception. Sloth (weariness in fighting temptation, bored with prayer) often permits despairing self-abuse. (The best modern treatise on these is Fairlie, *The Seven Deadly Sins.*)

Personal Sin

Sin is the conscious and deliberate violation of the moral law in intention or actual deed. A deliberate statement contrary to what I know to be true is the sin of lying. To be guilty of sin in a serious or mortal manner is consciously to choose to violate an inviolable good, after sufficient reflection and full consent of the will. When I deliberately wish to kill someone (and not the sudden urge to hurt which is immediately repressed) I am guilty of murder, whether I carry out the desire or not (for fear of being caught and punished). When I wish to experience orgasm alone, and not merely subjected to an involuntary erection and ejaculation on the edge of consciousness or during sleep, I am guilty of a serious sin of unchastity, because of the reserved nature of total mutual sexual self-gift which is sexual intercourse.

A true sense of guilt is a good thing! To call a conscious sin a mere error or mistake, a product of one's environment, a psychic compulsion because one does not feel sufficiently loved is not only false but is a positive insult to the sinner! It is to consider him, and help him to be, a psychopath! One cannot praise a person for a free good act, if one cannot blame a person for deliberate evil. "The buck (for praise or blame) stops here!" Though children, adolescents, and adults repeatedly search for and invent excuses for themselves, they all demand justice against others. It is incredibly true that thieves demand honesty and a fair share of the loot from their companions in crime!

Conscience

Conscience is a clear judgment based on objective truths that a certain act proposed for choice is morally obligatory or prohibited. Conscience is not a matter of imposing my own arbitrary idea upon reality. If an innocent human being is absolutely inviolable, then I may not directly kill him whether unborn, new-born, or long-born. Every truth forms, binds, my conscience! When the doctor tells me that my diet must be controlled for my diabetes, he binds my conscience. Nor may I insist that I may follow whatever I choose to do because "my conscience is clear." I do not get to plead "not guilty" with any conviction when I am cited for driving at 100 miles per hour on the open highway.

For a Christian and Catholic, conscience must be formed by the Teaching Church, as my medical conscience must be formed by my doctor (the word means teacher!). A Catholic cannot claim to be conscientiously pro-choice, conscientiously practicing sodomy, fornication, or marital contraception. Freedom of conscience does not mean that one makes up one's own rules, but that one ought not to be placed under unreasonable duress in doing what is right. The threat of a $100 fine for driving 15 miles above the speed-limit does not destroy freedom of conscience! My sense of obligation not to risk my life or the lives of others binds my conscience, and I freely follow that obligation!

Confession

The sacrament of penance or of reconciliation demands auricular confession to an actually listening ordained priest with faculties, who must actually judge, assign penance and absolve, unless some emergency intervenes, and then with the obligation of personally submitting to the keys those sins forgiven in the unusual situation. The penitent provides his own accusation and attempts to name the sin, its degree of guilt, the number of times performed, and any circumstances which might change its nature (e.g. a masturbatory act by a married person is quite different from one performed by an unmarried one). In case of doubt, the priest confessor must help resolve the doubt. The penitent also must protest his sorrow and purpose of amendment, and the priest must again judge the validity of this protest. If the sin has done notable harm to another, restitution for the damage must be demanded and promised by the penitent. The obligation to perform the assigned penance is serious, and failure to do so is a matter for a future confession.

Sometimes one wonders about the new designation of this sacrament as the sacrament of reconciliation. At times, in family or public life, a reconciliation is affirmed by the two parties merely letting "bygones be bygone" without either member admitting deliberate responsibility, guilt, sorrow, forgiveness, restoration, amendment, restitution. Such "reconciliation" is not provided by Christ or the Church. Though our sins are satisfied for ahead of time by the crucifixion of Christ, the fruits of His satisfaction cannot go into effect without the dispositions of the penitent. Indeed, His sacrificial death wins even the grace of sorrow for the sinner!

Penance and the approach to penance must be learned and practiced from earliest years. Any mother will attest the viciousness of children (or even to her own angers and nasty unfairness!) The drama, *The Bad Seed,* about a pre-school murderess, is eerily convincing. The Church demands that first penance precede first communion, even though one would hardly expect serious or mortal sins of those who are just emerging into the ability to judge right from wrong. This should not be surprising. The eucharist is a sacrifice for sin! Any one who cannot experience sorrow for sin is not capable of participating in that sacrifice!

The Confessor

If we insist on the freedom of a person to control his life, and recognize the scientific and public facts about the frequency of sexual sin, then we must teach frequency of approach to the sacrament of penance. Freedom demands responsibility for evil actions performed, and, therefore, guilt, sorrow, penance, restitution. It is a strange denial of human freedom that despite admitted multiple orgasm, fewer and fewer of us confess, and priests provide fewer and fewer opportunities for penance.

It is important to suggest to adolescents in particular that they find a regular confessor (the same one) who can act as a spiritual director, especially in two cases: 1) when one is struggling with a habit of sin; and 2) when one is considering the choice of a state in life (matrimony, celibacy, pursuing a call from a bishop to be a priest). Today we seem to go for counseling on the psychological level. The confessional does not provide that kind of time, but untold millions of Catholics have been helped to change their bitterness, hatreds, angers, blasphemies, backbiting, dishonesties, thefts, frauds, compulsions of intoxicating drink, drugs, and sex — long before we discovered the principles of Alcoholics (Overeaters, etc.) Anonymous, which are founded on Christian principles of recognition, confession, correction of and restitution for sin.

Children and adolescents (often adults!) are easily discouraged by failure. It is important to teach them that frequent falls are the fruit of a fallen human nature. Teachers as well as parents must be sympathetic and consoling, not harshly critical and rejective. Yet the only disaster is either the desire to wallow in sinfulness or the despairing refusal to try any further. Ask any alcoholic and he will tell you that he is always on the point of failure, that "easy does it," that he must live one day at a time, and that he must always be ready to start afresh. A wise and spiritual confessor will assign a regime of prayer, self-discipline, confidence in God, devotion to Our Lady to overcome any habit of sin.

Though it is possible that objectively sinful practices might be so compulsory as to be without subjective guilt, one cannot permit himself, or be permitted by advisors or confessors, to consider the practice of sinful actions as "good enough" or even virtuous in the sinner's situation. The habitual drunkard or drug abuser might not be guilty of every intoxication, but he cannot accept either as an acceptable and happy life-style. He must work at the famous 12 Steps of AA which have been adapted to, and adopted by, all addicts or compulsives: bulimics, liars, kleptomaniacs, cleanliness freaks, masturbators, pornography addicts, fornicators, sodomites, etc., etc.

Sacrament of the Sick

At first sight the explanation of this sacrament seems to suggest little of help for chastity and modesty. However, it is the final sacrament of the sacramentality of the body. The human body is not merely a house for an individual spirit or ego, or an instrumental mechanism for effects in a material world by a spiritual soul. It has inherent value and significance in itself and in all its human manifestations. This is the sacrament which is designed to cure the body of its ills and to prepare it to share finally and effectively in the resurrection of Jesus Christ. In the old ritual for anointing, the various senses (lips, ears, nose, hands and feet) were anointed, recognizing that these senses were intrinsically involved in the moral and spiritual life. The old formula was: "May the Lord forgive you by this holy anointing + and His most loving mercy whatever sins you have committed by the use of your sight (hearing, sense of smell, power of speech, sense of touch, power of walking)." In some realistic and open cultures of history, the genitals too were anointed, as persons faced dangerous illness. One wonders whether we might freshly examine these "curious" practices of the past. If the anointing of the sick is for the cure of illness, surely the epidemic spread of venereal disease through sinful activity could come into consideration for a sacrament of curing illness.

Miscellaneous Topics Which Come Up In The Class Room

Homosexuality

There are certain ways in which the human person is properly ordered or disposed. He naturally wishes to be self-aware and free for good judgment and wise choice. We call this good disposition sobriety. We recognize intoxication or drunkenness as depersonalizing when we feel embarrassed at being "out of one's gourd." At times we boast of the fun of being drunk or even "high on drugs," but we often look back with shame wondering what kind of fools we made of ourselves while "stoned." We recognize that the lack of judgment that intoxication brings makes us silly and dangerous. So we do not suggest that we do anything but say **no** to excessive drinking, **no** to merely euphoric drugs, even **no** to good drugs which can be abused (e.g. even aspirin!). A similarly proper disposition regarding speech and knowledge tell us that it is wrong to lie, to be misled, seduced with false advertising, betrayed. If we are addicted to anything like this, and are therefore unfree, we recognize that our "orientation" to abuse is not merely an option or freely chosen life-style. We recognize our need for the remedies against habitual sin in these areas, or, if we think we are helpless in the grip of addiction, we know we need help, therapy, operant conditioning, salutary fear, warnings (e.g. on cigarette packages and drugs), encouraging friends to share our concern and support our efforts to correct ourselves.

The proper way to be disposed or ordered in the area of sexuality is toward the opposite or correlative sex. The construction of the psychology and physiology of male and female and of masculine and feminine (as attributes of persons and not merely of functional bodies) suggests the significance of mutual spousal gift and receipt of love-union with openness to conception of a child. All other ways of achieving release are disoriented, disordered, though possibly compulsive (cf. above, The

Meaning of Sexual Intercourse). Heterosexual spousal orientation is considered normative in scripture and the teaching of the Church.

Normality is not a statistical average. Normality refers to the way things are designed and ought to be, even if the norm is seldom achieved. That most people lie from time to time never makes lying normal. That most people often have constipation or diarrhea never makes the sufferer feel *normal*. It is normal, correctly ordered, for a boy to be attracted sexually for a sexual romance which will found a life-commitment called marriage and matrimony (the word means "office of making a mother").

The mechanism of sexual arousal depends upon various kinds of psychological and/or physical stimulus, and automatic or learned response. Many men and women find themselves sexually stimulated by various techniques and scenarios. Some of these are stumbled upon, some learned from others, some seem to flow from no determined source but seem spontaneous and congenital. Some persons of either sex find themselves libidinously or erotically (see above) drawn to their own sex, and positively repelled by the opposite sex. No one seems to know the proportion of the population who suffer from this anomaly. It has been estimated as high as 10%, but this figure is disputed. The truth is further confused in that sexual stimulus can be completely amorphous (without any form or shape) for a long time, or in special situations where appetite is strong and only one's own sex is present, temporarily or for a long time. Freud thought that young children were "polymorphously perverse" since he recognized that orientation to procreating specified the truly normal and defined sexual perversity as departure from orientation to begetting.

At all events, Sacred Scripture and the Magisterium of the Church teach that homosexuality in orientation or practice is "intrinsically disordered" though only free and responsible practice of homosexual orgasm is considered sinful (cf. I Cor 6:9; SCDF *Declaration Concerning Sexual Ethics*, ¶ 10).

In the dictionary, the word "gay" is defined as meaning "full of mirthful or exuberant excitement." Homosexuals, especially male homosexuals, have been dubbed, and now willingly co-opt, the word **gay** to designate their attraction toward and libidinous actions with members of their own sex. They oppose this to *straight* (the word means direct, without deviation, unbent, correctly ordered, true) of heterosexual orientation. **Gay** seems more adapted to male homosexuality, while Lesbian refers to female homosexuality. The word "homophobic" has been invented to indicate any opposition to homosexuality as an arbitrary option of an acceptable "life-style" equivalent to marital heterosexuality. (Actually, the word in its dual root simply means "fear" of "the same.") A correctly rooted term would be "homosexuality phobia." Disapproval of any disorder need not be fearful or hating! No one who rejects the drug culture is accused of being pharmakeia-phobic (Greek for fear of potions).

Homosexuals argue that their orientation ought to be an acceptable preference, since otherwise they would be "doomed to celibacy." For a Catholic, we are all "doomed" to celibacy till such time as we can enter into the mutual marital commitment to one member of the opposite sex, unless we have chosen the spousal commitment to God in religious life or priesthood.

An organization for Catholic homosexuals is called Dignity. Generally, the group insists that active homosexual practice ought to be acceptable in the Catholic Church and that they should be permitted to have Mass celebrated for them at which they can participate at the holy table. This has been clearly forbidden by decrees from the various Roman Congregations. There is no reason that homosexuals should be excluded from the church, but unchastity of any kind precludes the reception of the sacraments of the living. Another organization for Catholic homosexuals is called Courage, which is an organization whose members pursue chastity with the overall philosophy used by Alcoholics Anonymous. This organization is fully approved by the Church in America and is quite successful.

Certainly, there should be no unjust discrimination against homosexuals, any more than there should be such discrimination against any one with an orientation against any healthy norm. We do not discriminate in job hiring against smokers, though we do discriminate against their smoking in the work place and perhaps demand an increase in their insurance premiums! However, the Church and Catholic schools must insist that homosexual life-style neither be taught or imaged positively in the educational or parental situation. The civic and religious communities ought to provide social support, benefits and approval for good family life of mother, father, one's own or correctly adopted children. Indeed, social good order demands positive discrimination in favor of such healthy families, which are the fundamental building blocks of the social order, and the only buffer between the arbitrary weight of state government and the chaotic disorders of individualism.

Venereal Diseases

This topic will inevitably come up in the upper grades. In the past it has been accepted that several diseases were spread by sexual activity. Their number was originally considered small, but now there are uncountable numbers. They have always been associated with unchaste promiscuity, and it is still true that if virginal partners were to remain faithful to each other for life, and such fidelity became universally desirable, these diseases would disappear within one or two generations, since even if contracted innocently, they eventually sterilize if not cured medically.

But these diseases have become so epidemic and usual that they have been renamed Sexually Transmitted Diseases (STD's). It seems that this new terminology has been invented to give the impression of innocent transmission. It is true that such diseases can be transmitted within marriage, but only if they have been contracted by previous and promiscuous sinful activity, or rarely, by transmission through the placenta or birth as an infant.

Aids (Acquired Immuno-Deficiency Syndrome)

Aids is a disease which suppresses the defensive system against other diseases of the human body. It is an acquired disease, acquired from someone who is carrying a virus called **HIV** (Human Immunodeficiency Virus). It is usually a sexually transmitted disease, though it can be transmitted through any intermingled body fluids of two or more persons — blood, semen, plasma. It is most often transmitted through heterosexual or homosexual sodomy, intravenous drug use with needles infected from a HIV carrier, blood contact with open lesions, transfer to unborn babies through the placenta, and (rarely today) blood transfusions. At the present moment it is incurable, and infected persons most often die within several years of discovery.

Aids has been introduced into humans by objectively disordered behavior, whether sexual promiscuity or drug abuse. It is therefore transmitted (originally at least) by objectively immoral social behavior. Though its spread into the general community may be innocent in individual cases, the origin of the disease always involved immoral behavior at some point in the chain of transfer. Though fear of venereal diseases in general and of **Aids** in particular will hardly motivate adolescents to chastity and modesty, it is nevertheless true that the only way to avoid **Aids** infection and **Aids** deaths is to remain virginal (and drug free) and to marry another virginal person and remain faithful to the commitment (cf. McIlhaney with Nethery, *1250 Health Care Questions Women Ask* [Grand Rapids, MI: Baker 1985] 626-630; McIlheney, *Sexuality and Sexually Transmitted Diseases* [Grand Rapids, MI: Baker, 1990].)

A great deal of love and compassion should be extended to those ill with **Aids**, and ordinary civil rights should not be denied them, nor opportunities to work, to earn a living, to take a part in society, etc. Further, Catholics should be especially concerned with the provision of health care as they have in all the plagues and health disasters of the past. However, **Aids** is an infectious disease, and society must take some defensive measures. We even demand that tubercular older persons do not live with their families in which young children are present, until such times as their disease is rendered less infectious. **Aids** sufferers may be socially limited in whatever activities might spread the disease. They certainly have the obligation, at minimum, to warn any innocent (or guilty) sexual partner of their condition, as well as remove themselves from such activities which might spread this disease. We already punish drug addicts for transferring their addiction to their unborn babies!

Beware of calling any sufferer a "victim." Generally, we concede victim status only to someone who has been affected by some *unjust* activity by another. I call myself a victim of rape or theft. I hardly can assert that I am a victim of the damage I do myself while DUI (Driving Under [intoxicating] Influence).

Safe Sex

This phrase seems to mean sexual experience (usually some sort of intercourse) without any un-pre-programmed results. Today it seems to mean sexual intercourse without commitment to a partner (no strings!), (unreversed) pregnancy, venereal disease, or effects other than the pre-planned (with the right to reverse after one changes his mind!). There is no such thing as "safe" sex, sexual union without irreversible consequences. The sexual act signifies and effects total and unconditional surrender to whatever might happen. Human beings unconsciously want it that way. Sex, even in marriage, is inherently "Risky Business."

The agonies of unrequited or unfaithful love are the stuff of almost all literature, drama, poetry. The few who succeed in avoiding entanglement end up utterly empty.

Sexual intercourse can never be made free from the risk of pregnancy, without or within marriage. Both the psychology and physiology of heterosexual partners trick them into pregnancy when they experience "method" or "patient" failures (failure of contraceptive *method;* failure to *use* contraception). The records of the Guttmacher Institute (the "research arm" of Planned Parenthood) admit that the more contraception that is made available, the more knowledgeable are its users, there are more unwanted pregnancies, more unwed mothers, the more abortions, the more infancticides of the handicapped, the more battered and rejected children.

Safe sex does not work in correcting venereal disease. All such disease have geometrically multiplied since the early introduction of "safe" methods in the military during the First World War, and we now count some 25-30 sexually transmitted diseases. A ghoulish teenage joke: "What's the difference between herpes and marriage?" "**Herpes** is forever!"

Obscenity

Every teacher must come to grips with "earthy" language. It might be of value to help growing young people to distinguish three kinds of unacceptable language: vulgarity, the bawdy and obscenity.

Vulgarity embraces those words for bodily processes and their results which are not used in polite society, or in the public forum. There is nothing particularly against chastity and modesty in their use. Their offensiveness is against politeness, respect for others, obedience to parents, courtesy to fellows. At times, as expletives, they are diffusive of anger, frustration, exasperation. They may even have some harmless shock value. But more often they reveal utter inadequacy in vocabulary, and proportionality to the situation. Unfortunately, they have become so universal on the large and small screen, that they seem to have little more meaning than a comma in a written sentence!

The bawdy involves references to sexual sinfulness in a light and humorous manner, or even to a marital sexual experience in a way which defuses its awesome seriousness. Generally the bawdy should be private, but it is often used as a foil for seriousness in drama and musical comedy. Dolittle in "My Fair Lady" can boast that with "A lit'l bit o' luck" he will not get "hooked" in his philandering. But this is a foil for the gradual and serious love-hate-love relationship between Eliza and 'enry 'iggins. Ado Annie in "Oklahoma!" brings the house down with "I Cain't Say NO." But she eventually snares a boy who found "everything up to date in Kansas City," against the beauty of "Let People Say We're in Love." Teenagers can be taught to laugh at the dangers and failures of unchastity while still pursuing their reality.

Obscenity is something else again. It is the use of offensive, demeaning and lustful language, especially to denigrate love-union as so much instrumental, mechanical or animalistic rutting. Our teenagers must be taught to judge this material as they cannot help hearing it from the modern screen in movies from which they are supposed to be excluded ("R!"), but where they are most often found. But "Dirty Words Can Hurt You!" Obscenity destroys the user as well as the one upon whom it is used.

The above could be a helpful class study of language or literature. There is so much vulgarity and bawdiness in Shakespeare, but very little if any obscenity (cf. Thomas Howard, *Chance or the Dance*, 120-121).

Sexism

The suffix "ism" can mean a number of things: it can indicate a body of truths or doctrines on a certain topic or of a certain group (Catholicism, individualism, Americanism); it can mean a legitimate preference of one thing over another (vegetarianism); it can mean an unjust or unfair discrimination in favor of one thing to the positive harm to the other (a racism which refuses legitimate employment to a member of a group because of racial or ethnic preference). Unfortunately the suffix in today's parlance almost always suggests some injustice demanding civil, legal, or communal redress, with penalty against the discriminator.

Any body of defensible truths must discriminate against all opposites in order to defend and promote itself. The commission of Christ to the

Apostles (and through them to us) to go into the whole world and preach the "Good News" means that we must profess orthodoxy, preach *all* the revealed truths, defend those truths, attempt to persuade all men to embrace them, protect our faith and our communicants from all other "faith-systems." This is the reason we have Catholic and not non-denominational churches, the reason for Catholic schools, the reason we demand assent to these truths from those who lead or teach in either (at least not public opposition or dissent founding rebellion or dissolution of our faith).

Discrimination on the basis of objective truth is the foundation of all freedom, and of all choice! I cannot be free unless I can discriminate between one thing and another. I am not free if I am compelled to take a politically meaningless position. I cannot choose unless I judge that one alternate is to be preferred to the other. I discriminate against homosexuality when I insist that my sexual partner must be a person of the opposite sex for a lifetime with openness to begetting. I am not practicing unjust discrimination when I insist that my familyism demands that only mother, father and their own children (along with blood relatives) can form and be counted as a family, and not a menage of sorority, fraternity, or coed living arrangements, or homosexual menage *à trois* or more. I am not *guilty* of "speciesism" but positively proud to be a speciesist when I insist that plants, fish and animals have been give to me to "husband" and to provide for my nourishment, service, rational use! I discriminate. On occasion I have good reason to kill and eat a chicken. I can never kill and eat a baby.

Sexism should mean the body of truths concerning the differences between men and women. Scripture and the teaching of the Church have consistently taught that there are intrinsic and not merely incidental differences between men and women. What these might be can be disputed in various cases, as well as how they are to be socially taught, but that they exist ought not be denied. It is strange that some radical feminists often are not asserting a value for femininity but an opposition to masculinity, in order to destroy the virile, and take its place. It is a further anomaly that women seeking an abortion for the sake of sexual preference, often prefer to bear boy babies and kill girl babies!

At all events, a major psychological problem today is the maturation of children in the appropriation of masculinity or femininity, especially in these days of unmarried mothers, divorce, separation, absent or ineffectual fathers. It is strongly suggested in much psychological literature that failure to identify with the parent of one's own sex and to contrast oneself with the parent of the opposite sex is the source of manifold emotional difficulties and the possible cause of homosexual orientation (cf. Ruth T Barnhouse, *Homosexuality: A Symbolic Confusion* [New York: Seabury, 1977]).

As a result of this conviction, the maximum number of truly masculine and feminine models should be provided for both sexes in Catholic schools. Pius XI in his famous encyclical on Catholic education (*Divini Illius Illustri*, Dec. 31, 1929) inveighed against co-education when understood as identical and interchangeable formation of boys and girls. This is what we might call uni-sex education (an oxymoron!) today. Catholic schools today may well be female ridden. In most of our schools there are few if any male teachers until high school. It is suggested that girls need formation by males as well as do boys! (Cf. George Gilder, *Men and Marriage*, [Gretna, L: Pelican, 1986]; with reservations, Walter Ong, *Fighting For Life* [Ithaca, NY: Cornell, 1981]; Robert Bly, *Iron John* [Reading, MA: Addison-Wesley, 1990]; Deborah Tannen, *You Just Don't Understand* [New York: Morrow, 1990].)

It is indeed necessary to discover, name and root out all injustices to both men and women, boys and girls. But it is necessary first to recognize, define and promote intrinsic sexual differences. It should be clear that the refusal of maternal sacramentality of body and mind by radical feminists, and the rush to escape virile initiative and responsibility by our Peter Pan males is destroying the family. If true sexual formation is not rediscovered, our individualistic liberalism for both sexes will leave only atomistic personal monads facing the bureaucratic impersonal dictatorship. The family will disappear and the Brave New World will become a reality.